CODE BREAKERS

FROM HIEROGLYPHS TO HACKERS

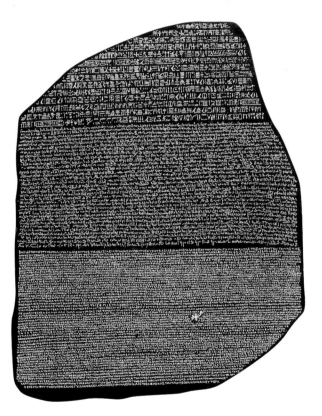

CODE BREAKERS
FROM HIEROGLYPHS TO HACKERS

By
Simon Adams

Consultant
Peter Chrisp

A Dorling Kindersley Book

LONDON, NEW YORK, MUNICH,
MELBOURNE, and DELHI

Project Editor David John
Designer Darren Holt
Senior Editor Fran Jones
Senior Art Editor Stefan Podhorodecki
Category Publisher Jayne Parsons
Managing Art Editor Jacquie Gulliver
Picture Researcher Sean Hunter
DK Pictures Sally Hamilton
Production Erica Rosen
DTP Designer Siu Yin Ho
Jacket Designer Dean Price

First American Edition, 2002

02 03 04 05 10 9 8 7 6 5 4 3 2 1

Published in the United States by
DK Publishing, Inc.
95 Madison Avenue
New York, NY 10016

A Cataloging-in-Publication record for this title
is available from the Library of Congress

ISBN 0-7894-8529-X (HC)
ISBN 0-7894-8530-3 (PB)

Reproduced by Colourscan, Singapore
Printed and bound by L.E.G.O., Italy

See our complete product line at

www.dk.com

CONTENTS

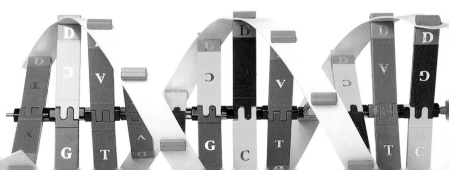

INTRODUCTION

Few of us can resist a mystery. Once we're intrigued, we want to search for clues until we've solved the puzzle. No wonder then that secret codes are among the most fascinating mysteries of all. Some take years of code breaking before they give up the secrets hidden inside their numbers, letters, or symbols.

Codes are as old as civilization itself. People have been inventing codes for as long as they've had information to keep secret – and that's a long time! Kings, queens, popes, and emperors encoded personal and diplomatic messages to keep their intrigues hidden from spies and foreign powers. Lovers wrote coded letters to each other to keep their meetings secret. Military leaders gave coded orders to prevent vital intelligence from falling into enemy hands. At first, these codes involved no more than a simple juggling of the alphabet. But by the 16th century, some

WHEEL-CIPHERS ENCODED MESSAGES BY ALIGNING THE LETTERS ON TWO ROTATING DISCS.

codes were so complex
that they were almost
impossible to break. As
code makers invented
ever more difficult codes,
so code breakers became
more sophisticated at
cracking them. And by World War II, the
first computers were being built to crack the
Germans' Enigma – the most unbreakable
code machine the world had ever seen.

NOT ALL CODES ARE SECRET. ONE OF THE MOST COMMON CODES USED TODAY IS THE LANGUAGE OF TEXT MESSAGING.

CAN U DCODE A TXT MSSGE? :-)

   The contest between code makers and breakers
remains as fierce today as ever, as hackers continue to
find a way through the codes protecting all manner of
sensitive secrets. For the moment, however, the code
makers have the upper hand. We've reached an age
where truly unbreakable codes are used every day.
These may never be cracked until a whole new
generation of computers is invented. This book tells
the story of code breaking from ancient times to the
present age of quantum science. You'll find out about
some of the most complicated codes ever devised
and the billiant people who cracked them.

   If you'd like to explore the subject in more detail,
there are "Log On" boxes that appear throughout the
book. These will direct you to some fascinating
websites where you can
check out even more
about codes and code
breaking.

Simon Adams

LIFE'S A CODE

Think of codes and code breaking, and you think of spies and wartime adventures, or secret messages that lead to hidden fortunes. But think a little more and you soon realize that codes are part of daily life. That's because there are two types of code – one to keep information secret, and one to communicate it openly, at home, at work, and even in the street. Indeed, most of us make and break codes every day of our lives.

Communicating in code

Take the words on this page. If you read English, you understand what each word means. But if you are French, or Chinese, these words will make no sense at all unless you can also read English. Language is a type of code, shared only by those who can understand that language. In the case of English, the code is shared by 1.4 billion people around the world, so it's hardly a secret!

But, as we shall see later, only a few thousand people speak the Native American Navajo language. People who are not native Navajos can't understand a single word of it.

E veryday codes

Every time you use a computer, you use a code. Computers speak in a special number code, and without this code the machine on your desk would not work. It certainly would not be able to "talk" to other computers around the world via the internet. When you use your home telephone, you need an area code to make sure you get connected to the number you want in Manhattan rather than in Minneapolis or Missoula. And when you send a letter, you use a zip code to identify the address correctly.

Codes can also take the form of symbols or pictures. The green traffic light that allows you to drive on, and the red light that

GRAFFITI CAN BE A CODE THAT ONLY CERTAIN GROUPS OF PEOPLE, SUCH AS MEMBERS OF A GANG, WILL UNDERSTAND.

tells you to stop are codes. So, too, is the color code that stops your mom or dad from wiring a plug the wrong way, or the laundry symbol that tells them not to tumble dry your best shirt!

Even clothes are a type of code that indicate to others what sort of person you are. Fashion codes must constantly change. If too many people "crack" them, then the clothes become unfashionable.

In short, codes are part of our everyday lives, so much so that we take them for granted. Without codes, life would be much more confusing.

Defining a code

At this point, we need some definitions. Technically speaking, a code replaces a whole word or phrase with a letter, number, or symbol. On the other hand, a cipher

COMPUTERS SPEAK TO EACH OTHER WITH A SPECIAL NUMBER SYSTEM CALLED BINARY CODE, MADE UP OF THE DIGITS 0 AND 1.

replaces the individual letters of a word. Thus, the code for "Florida" could be the single letter X or number 28, while the cipher for "Florida" has six letters or numbers, such as BAFWAFZ or 61 9 45 13 9 45 8. You use a code to encode a message, and then decode it to make sense again. Likewise, you encipher and decipher a message using ciphers. The science of encoding a message is called cryptography. Breaking a code or cipher is called cryptanalysis.

Confused? Well, don't be, because today the difference between codes and ciphers is increasingly blurred. For the sake of simplicity and an easy life, let's just call them all codes, unless there is a good reason to be more precise.

S ecret codes

So why use secret codes? In history, as we shall see, the first codes were invented to safeguard military secrets. A messenger taking an important order from a commander to his troops on the battlefield might be captured and the message fall into enemy hands. This would put the lives of the troops in danger. Write the message in a code, however, and the instruction could be kept secret.

Codes were also invented to safeguard national secrets, such as a letter to a foreign leader proposing an alliance to attack a common enemy, or the details of a plot to assassinate a neighboring king. Even routine diplomatic letters from ambassadors were written in code to keep their contents safe. Ingenious Greeks and Romans, Arabs and Europeans, emperors and kings,

WRITING IS A CODE FOR COMMUNICATING – AS LONG AS YOU KNOW THE LANGUAGE. YOU WOULD NEED TO UNDERSTAND JAPANESE TO READ THESE COMICS.

Mr. David John
Dorling Kindersley
95 Madison Avenue
New York, NY 10016

devised ever-more complex codes to protect their military and state secrets from enemy eyes.

The secret code industry

For every person who devised a code, another was employed to break it. By the 19th century, teams of code breakers routinely opened diplomatic mailbags and intercepted foreign-bound messages in an attempt to discover what their country's enemies were up to. Code making and code breaking became big business, and its employees were experts.

Safe and secure

Today, codes for privacy and security are used by everybody, not just leaders and armies. Technology has made codes cheap and sophisticated. You can encrypt your emails with virtually unbreakable codes downloaded free from the internet. Banks and businesses can talk to each other privately through their computer networks. They elecronically

WEIRD WORLD

THE PRESIDENTS OF THE US AND RUSSIA COMMUNICATE VIA A TELEPHONE "HOTLINE" DURING EMERGENCIES. SO SECRET ARE THEIR CONVERSATIONS THAT THEY USE A CODE, WHICH CHANGES EVERY DAY.

12

transfer money around the world in seconds. All these transactions are protected by security codes. Without them, money could be paid into the wrong bank account or commercial secrets might fall into the hands of a competitor. Military communications via satellite are also encrypted, as are telephone conversations between governments. Even the burglar alarm in your house or the intercom outside your front door has a code to prevent burglars from entering. Codes protect your house and your belongings and safeguard your money from fraud. They also protect your country and keep you safe from harm. Codes, in other words, are essential to our lives.

FASHION CODES ARE USED TO IDENTIFY WITH A CERTAIN GROUP OF PEOPLE, AND TO EXCLUDE OTHERS FROM THAT GROUP.

SIGNS OF THE TIMES

People have always used codes to convey information. In the distant past they used simple picture codes or signs to record data. These signs were not meant to be secret, but were designed to be easily understood. Every civilization has its own codes for communicating. Over time, their meanings are often lost or forgotten and can be so baffling to modern eyes that it takes the greatest code breakers to unlock them. The codes of our own civilization will probably be no different.

TEXT MESSAGING IS A DISCREET WAY TO PASS ON GOSSIP, SWAP JOKES, AND ARRANGE MEETINGS WITH YOUR FRIENDS – AND ITS ALL DONE IN CODE!

The world's favorite code
In a thousand years' time, your phone text messages may be as mysterious to future generations as certain ancient writing is to us today. That's assuming any examples of these messages survive. Technology now makes communicating in code rapid, cheap, and discreet. Want to send a message to a friend but they're in a class? Then you probably use your mobile phone to send text messages. You're not alone, because around the world, about 25 *billion* messages are sent every month! And every one of those people is talking in code. Text messaging is one of the most common codes for communicating today.

WAN2TLK?

There are hundreds of abbreviation codes mobile phone users key in when using the Short Message Service, as text messaging is properly known. Messages must be short because a mobile phone's screen can only fit 160 letters in languages such as English, French, and Spanish – that's a maximum of about 30 words – and only 70 letters in languages such as Chinese or Arabic.

Short and sweet

You've got to be really inventive to squeeze meaning into so few characters. You might

THX 4 BEING A GR8 FRIEND. C U 2MORO :-)

TEXT MESSAGES ARE A MIXTURE OF LETTERS, NUMBERS, AND SYMBOLS.

WEIRD WORLD

THE TEXT MESSAGING WORLD LEADER IS GERMANY, WHERE 1.8 BILLION TEXT MESSAGES WERE SENT IN DECEMBER 2000. THE WHOLE OF EUROPE SENT 7 BILLION MESSAGES THAT MONTH.

say CUL8R (see you later), LOL (lots of love), 2NITE (tonight), TX (thanks) and even OXOXOXO (hugs and kisses). These are just some of the codes in everyday use, but you and your fellow texters have no doubt invented many more.

Easy and fun

Most text codes use the first letter of each word (ATB = all the best) or shorten a word using single letters in place of a syllable (EZ = easy). Some use numbers in place of syllables or simple words (2 = to) or combine letters and numbers (B4 = before). You may even tell your friends what frame of mind you're in by using pictures made from punctuation

15

marks, viewed sideways. These are called emoticons and there are a growing number of them used for fun. There's **:-)**, to say you're happy, or **:-o**, to mean "oops," and even **@:-(** (I don't like my new hairstyle).

P icture this

The advantage of using pictures as codes is that they can be understood by anybody. Pictures overcome the barriers of language. Some picture codes in use today have very obvious meanings, such as the sign that says you can't smoke.

THIS DANGEROUS-LOOKING SYMBOL MEANS BIOHAZARD. TRIANGLES ARE USUALLY WARNING SIGNS.

Some are well known, such as the red cross that tells you a vehicle is an ambulance. But others require decoding and some understanding of what they mean. The international yellow hazard signs are designed to be understood worldwide, but not all of them are immediately obvious. If you see one with three fans coming out of a black dot, stay away. It means radioactive!

C hoose a symbol

Because not everyone can read and write, picture codes are often used instead of letters. For example, in an election, you are given a ballot paper with the names of the candidates on it. In many countries, including India, South Africa, and the UK, those names are accompanied by a symbol to show which party the candidate belongs to. The wheel represents the Indian Congress Party, the rose the British Labour Party, and so on. People who can't read the names can look for their candidate's party symbol.

E arly signs

There's nothing new about using pictures as a code for giving information. For thousands of years, people painted pictures in caves and left messages in simple picture signs because the alphabets we use today were unknown. This was more effective than you may think. A single image can contain a lot of information.

In about 3300 BC, the ancient

A VOTER IN AN SOUTH AFRICAN GENERAL ELECTION EXAMINES THE CANDIDATES' PARTY SYMBOLS.

peoples of Mesopotamia, who lived in what is now Iraq, developed a form of writing based on simple drawings of the world around them. Each pictogram, as they are known, represented a word or idea. An outline of a cow's head represented "cow," while the harvest. Later, they recorded the history of the country and its kings. Pictograms were a universal code. It did not matter what language you spoke – you could still decode the pictures.

SOME ANCIENT SCRIPTS STILL DEFY ALL ATTEMPTS AT CODE BREAKING

combined signs for woman and mountains represented a foreign woman from over the mountains, meaning a female slave.

Pictograms were first used to keep records of the annual

Words in wedges

The Mesopotamian scribes used a reed stylus (a little like a modern fountain pen, but without the ink) to scratch these pictograms into wet clay tablets. These were then dried

17

in the sun. Because it is easier to cut a straight line into wet clay than a curved one, pictograms evolved into a series of wedge-shaped straight lines. The name for this writing is cuneiform, from the Latin word *cuneus*, meaning wedge.

MAYAN GLYPHS WERE DRAWN INSIDE OVALS, CIRCLES, OR SQUARES.

WEIRD WORLD

THE ONE PLACE IN THE WORLD WHERE PICTURE WRITING SURVIVES IS CHINA. CHINESE WRITING USES MORE THAN 50,000 PICTOGRAMS, ALTHOUGH MOST PEOPLE NEED ONLY A FEW THOUSAND FOR EVERYDAY USE.

Riddle of the glyphs

Centuries later, in about AD 300, on the other side of the world, the Mayan people of Central America developed their own pictograms. After the Maya disappeared, the meanings of their glyphs, or pictures, remained secret until 1980. Researchers then realized that the complex pictures were combinations of whole ideas and single sounds, while bars

THE PICTOGRAM FOR BEER IS AN UPTURNED JUG WITH A POINTED BASE.

CUNEIFORM WAS A FORM OF PICTURE WRITING THAT WAS USED TO WRITE SEVERAL ANCIENT LANGUAGES.

A SQUARE-ENDED STYLUS MAKES TRIANGULAR SHAPES.

THE AZTECS RECORDED THE DEEDS OF GODS AND HEROES IN PICTURE STORIES. A SHIELD AND A CLUB REPRESENTED WAR. A BURNING TEMPLE REPRESENTED VICORY.

and dots represented numbers. By drawing glyphs of gods, births, deaths, and battles, the Maya accurately recorded their people's history.

Aztec days

The Maya's neighbors, the Aztecs, ruled what is now Mexico from the 1200s onward. They used pictures to draw up their highly complex calendars. Like the Maya, the Aztecs were obsessed with the passage of time and had a glyph for each day of the month and each month of the year. Just as we number the days of our months from 1 to 30 or 31, the Aztecs depicted their days by drawing a flower, rain, a knife, or an alligator.

Unlocking the past

Even today, ancient picture scripts exist that refuse to give up their secrets. One sophisticated 4,000-year-old script from northern India has more than 400 different signs, and experts still have no idea what they mean. But thanks to the work of a brilliant young code breaker, we can read and understand the most mysterious ancient script of all time – hieroglyphs, the writing of ancient Egypt.

THE KEY TO EGYPT

Go to Egypt today and you will see the evidence of a great civilization all around you. Vast pyramids and temples stand out in the desert and the museums are full of artifacts. We know a lot about the ancient Egyptians, yet until quite recently there was a gap in our knowledge because no one could read their writing. Deciphering the Egyptians' ancient script is one of the greatest achievements in the history of code breaking.

The hieroglyph mystery

During the 18th century, Europeans visiting Egypt marveled at the fabulous remains of a long-vanished civilization. But they were puzzled by the strange picture writings they could not read. These were called hieroglyphs, from the Greek words meaning "sacred carvings." All knowledge of hieroglyphs had been lost for about 1,400 years, so scholars could only

HIEROGLYPHS WERE DEVELOPED IN ABOUT 3100 BC AND WERE USED UNTIL ABOUT 600 AD.

THE ROSETTA STONE

DEMOTIC WAS A SHORT FORM OF HIEROGLYPHS DEVELOPED FOR DAILY USE IN ABOUT 600 BC.

ANCIENT GREEK COULD BE READ BY SCHOLARS. THEY MATCHED ROYAL NAMES WRITTEN IN GREEK AND HIEROGLYPHS.

speculate about the meaning of the pictures. They assumed that each picture stood for a whole word or idea. For example, the hieroglyph of a hawk, a fast bird, meant "speed." But this was just guessing. All links to the language of the pharaohs had been broken long ago.

The Rosetta Stone

It wasn't until 1799, when the French army occupied Egypt, that a remarkable discovery was made that would finally unlock the mystery of hieroglyphs. Troops in Rosetta, a village in the Nile delta, uncovered a large black slab weighing three-

JEAN-FRANÇOIS CHAMPOLLION WAS THE GENIUS WHO FINALLY DECODED HIEROGLYPHS. BUT THE EFFORT RUINED HIS HEALTH AND HE DIED AT THE AGE OF 41.

quarters of a ton. It had three sets of writing on it. The top 14 lines were written in hieroglyphs. The middle 32 lines were written in a strange script called demotic, which was used by ancient Egyptian scribes for everyday business and as a quick shorthand alternative to hieroglyphs. Crucially, the bottom 54 lines were written in ancient Greek. Scholars quickly read the Greek text and discovered that the stone was

carved in 196 BC as a tribute to pharaoh Ptolemy V by priests thanking him for various favors. The scholars correctly guessed that the hieroglyphs and the demotic contained the same message. But before they could decipher them, the French were defeated by the

HIEROGLYPHS WERE DIFFICULT TO DRAW WELL. IN THE END THEY WERE ONLY USED FOR FORMAL PURPOSES.

British and were forced to hand over the stone. As a result, the Rosetta Stone, as it became known, ended up in the British Museum, London, where you can see it today.

The first breakthrough

Two remarkable men now enter the story. The first was Thomas Young (1773–1829), an English child prodigy and all-around genius. He could read by the age of 2 and by 14 could understand 12 foreign languages. In 1814, Young took a copy of the Rosetta Stone with him on vacation to the English seaside.

While there, he studied a set of hieroglyphs surrounded by a loop, or cartouche. He guessed that this represented someone

that certain hieroglyphs represented single letters or sounds, just like a modern aphabet. But he still believed the old view that most hieroglyphs represented whole words and ideas. Young wasn't very good at finishing the projects he'd started, and soon gave up.

PTOLEMAIOS IN HIEROGLYPHS

PTOLEMAIOS IN DEMOTIC

ΠΤΟΛΕΜΑΙΟΣ

PTOLEMAIOS IN GREEK

The fainting genius

The person who finally cracked this ancient code was a Frenchman, Jean-François Champollion (1790–1832). Like Young, Champollion was a child genius. He had been obsessed with hieroglyphics since he was very young and had learned 12 ancient languages to prepare himself for the challenge of

WEIRD WORLD

THOMAS YOUNG WAS A GENIUS IN OTHER FIELDS, INCLUDING OPTICS. BY PLACING METAL RINGS AROUND A LIVING HUMAN EYEBALL, HE PROVED THAT THE INTERNAL LENS DID THE FOCUSING, NOT THE WHOLE EYE!

important, possibly Ptolemy, since his name also appeared in the Greek text (where it is spelled Ptolemaios). What Young had stumbled upon was

deciphering the pictures. Among these languages was Coptic, which used the Greek alphabet. It had been introduced by the church when Egypt became Christian in the first centuries AD.

By studying different sets of inscriptions, he found the hieroglyphs for three names – Ptolemy, Cleopatra, the famous queen, and Alexander, who conquered Egypt in 332 BC.

However, all the names discovered so far were famous Greeks who had ruled Egypt. None of them was Egyptian. Champollion still did not know anything at all about the ancient Egyptian language.

The spell is broken

Champollion's amazing discovery came in 1822 when he was studying a stone carving from the temple of Abu Simbel. This temple dated from the

letter "S." The first symbol was a disc that resembled the sun. In an inspired guess, he wondered if the disc

THESE ARE THE HIEROGLYPHS FOR RAMESES II. HE WAS MENTIONED IN GREEK HISTORIES BUT NO ONE KNEW HOW GREAT HE WAS UNTIL HIS NAME WAS DECIPHERED AT ABU SIMBEL.

represented the Coptic for sun – the word (and single syllable) "RA." He now had "RA–SS." Champollion guessed that the missing letter was "M." He also guessed that the scribes had left out the vowels, as they often did in other ancient languages. If the missing vowels were "E," put it all together, and the cartouche spelt "RA-M-E-S-E-S," one of the

CHAMPOLLION WOULD FAINT IF HE GOT TOO WORKED UP

golden age of ancient Egypt and long before the period of Greek rule. He looked at a single cartouche containing four hieroglyphs. The last two symbols were the same and he knew each represented the

greatest pharaohs of all. "I've got it!" Champollion cried. But the excitement was too much. He fainted and had to spend five days in bed!

Champollion had broken the code. Not only had he discovered that hieroglyphs represented a mixture of whole words and single letters, but that ancient Egyptian and Coptic were one and the same language. Within two years he

almost every hieroglyph. It was now possible to read what the Egyptians wrote and hear the language they used. After 1,400 silent years, an ancient civilization was speaking again.

TWO OF THE FOUR COLOSSAL STATUES OF RAMESES II THAT STAND AT ABU SIMBEL.

WAR AND INTRIGUE

The history of making and breaking secret codes is as old as the history of warfare and diplomacy. Kings, queens, and emperors needed to protect state secrets from enemies, and generals wanted to pass orders safely to their troops. But each time the code makers invented a clever new system for disguising information, the code breakers would set about cracking it.

A SPARTAN MESSENGER DISGUISED THE STRIP AS A BELT OR BODY ARMOR.

THE MESSAGE COULD ONLY BE READ BY SOMEONE WITH THE SAME-SIZED SCYTALE.

The secret stick

An early military code was created more than 2,500 years ago, when ancient Greece was in a constant state of war. One particularly warlike city-state called Sparta was always fighting its neighbors. To send and receive military information in secret, the Spartans invented a "secret stick." This was the *scytale*, a multisided wooden stick, around which was wrapped a long strip of leather.

The message was written lengthwise along the *scytale*, across the strips of leather. When it was unwound, the long string of letters made no

S E N D M O R E
M E N U R G E N T

sense. The messenger carried the leather strip to the commander, who then wrapped it round his own *scytale* to read the message. Only a person with the same-sized *scytale* could read the message. Thanks to such a simple but effective system, major battles were won.

JULIUS CAESAR IS ONE OF HISTORY'S MOST BRILLIANT GENERALS. HIS CODE GAVE HIM A STRATEGIC ADVANTAGE OVER ROME'S ENEMIES.

Spartan scrabble

The Spartan *scytale* is a form of cipher in which the individual letters are transposed or mixed up. These transposed ciphers are really just scrambled words, or anagrams. Unscramble the anagrams and you decipher the message. By the way, the message to be put into code is called plaintext. In modern times, plaintext is always written without any capital letters. The ciphertext, or the coded message, is always written in CAPITALS.

The Caesar shift

A trickier form of cipher is substitution, where an individual letter is replaced by another letter. The most famous of these is the Caesar shift, so named because it was used by the Roman dictator, Julius Caesar (100–44 BC). The principle behind this is easy. Each letter of the alphabet is

WEIRD WORLD

THERE ARE MORE THAN 400,000,000,000,000,000, 000,000,000 (400 SEPTILLION) DIFFERENT WAYS TO ARRANGE A PLAINTEXT ALPHABET INTO A CIPHER ALPHABET!

replaced by another letter three, four, or whatever places down the alphabet. A Caesar shift of four places therefore turns a into E, b into F, and so on. Write out ZIRM ZMHM ZMGM and it makes no sense. But go back four places and Caesar's famous remark soon becomes

message, and suspecting use of the Caesar shift, would not take long to work through the 26 possible shifts (one for each other letter of the alphabet) before deciphering the message. Likewise, the repetition of VWX in a coded message might suggest a much-used three-letter word, such as "the"

IN 9TH-CENTURY BAGHDAD YOU COULD HAVE LEARNED ABOUT EVERYTHING FROM ASTRONOMY TO CRYPTOGRAPHY.

clear – Veni, vidi, vici ("I came, I saw, I conquered!").

or "and." The code breaker could then figure out what some letters were and then fill in the gaps for the others – a little like a crossword puzzle.

E asy to crack

However, Julius Caesar (and the secret diary writers among you) couldn't guarantee that the substitution cipher messages would remain secret. Anyone capturing a coded

T he science of secrecy

The people who turned the rough-and-ready art of code making into a science were the Arabs. From their capital city of Baghdad (in modern-day Iraq), the fabulous Abbasid dynasty established a powerful empire where commerce and culture flourished. They developed an efficient administrative system and for secrecy kept many of their records in code.

breakers learned new skills to break existing codes.

Frequency analysis

The greatest Arab code breaker was the 9th-century scientist

AN EXTRACT FROM AL-KINDI'S FAMOUS MANUSCRIPT ON DECIPHERING CRYPTOGRAPHIC MESSAGES.

Administrators followed rules laid down in the *Adab al-Kuttab* (*The Secretaries' Manual*), a 10th-century book with chapters on cryptography. At first, these code makers used simple transcription ciphers. Later they got more adventurous and devised substitution ciphers using signs such as + or # instead of letters. Working alongside them, code

Abu Yusuf Ya'qub ibn Is-haq ibn as-Sabbah ibn 'omran ibn Ismail al-Kindi, known as "the philosopher of the Arabs," or al-Kindi for short! He wrote 290 books on medicine, astronomy, mathematics, and other subjects, including *A Manuscript on Deciphering Cryptographic Messages*.

In the book, he made the simple observation that a good way to solve an encrypted message, if you know what language it was written in, is to find any page in a book written in the same language, and see which are the most-used letters. In English, the most frequently used letter is e, followed by t and a. Then look at the encrypted message, find the most frequently used symbol, and (if the orignial message was written in English) it probably represents the letter e. Find the

WEIRD WORLD

THE FIRST EUROPEAN INSTITUTIONS TO STUDY CRYPTANALYSIS WERE THE MONASTERIES, WHERE MONKS STUDIED THE BIBLE IN SEARCH OF HIDDEN MEANINGS.

29

second most common symbol, and that is probably t, and so on, through the alphabet using what is called frequency analysis until the coded message becomes clear.

The cruel cousin

If Mary, Queen of Scots had known something about frequency analysis, the history of Britain might have been very different. Mary, a Roman Catholic, become queen of Scotland in 1542 when she was just one week old. After falling out of favor with the Scottish nobles in 1568, she fled to England, where she hoped her cousin, Queen Elizabeth I, would give her a home. This was a terrible mistake.

Elizabeth, a Protestant, saw Mary as a dangerous threat and locked her up.

MARY WAS IMPRISONED FOR 18 YEARS IN A SERIES OF CASTLES. SHE WAS A PRIVILEGED PRISONER AND ALLOWED SOME FREEDOMS.

Plotting and scheming

From prison, Mary plotted to assassinate Elizabeth and seize the English throne. She began writing letters in code to her main supporter, Anthony Babington. Her cipher used 23 symbols that were substituted for letters of the alphabet (except for j, v, and w) and 36 symbols used to represent whole words. Unfortunately for Mary,

PHELIPPE'S FORGED LINES AT THE END OF MARY'S LETTER ASKED HER CORRESPONDENT TO REVEAL THE PLOTTERS' NAMES.

O	‡	∧	⧻	ɑ	⬜	θ	∞	I	♂	ϰ
A	B	C	D	E	F	G	H	I	K	L

II	∅	▽	ς	M	ƒ	△	Ɛ	c	7	8	9
M	N	O	P	Q	R	S	T	U	X	Y	Z

her letters were being opened by Elizabeth's spies, and passed to Thomas Phelippes, an expert code breaker. Phelippes quickly broke the code using frequency analysis. Thinking her code was safe, Mary was very unguarded about what she wrote. The letters revealed what Mary was up to, but not the names of the other conspirators.

MARY'S CIPHER USED A CODED ALPHABET AND SUBSTITUTION WORDS.

were arrested and suffered horrible deaths. Mary was tried for treason and beheaded on February 8, 1587.

The trap is set
Cunningly, Phelippes added a few lines to one of Mary's letters, in a perfect forgery of her handwriting. He asked Babington for the names of all the plotters. The letter was then delivered and Babington, not suspecting a trap, replied with the names.

The plotters

MARY'S LIFE ENDED ON THE BLOCK AFTER HER CONVICTION FOR TREASON.

THE VIGENÈRE SQUARE ALLOWED
PLAINTEXT TO BE ENCIPHERED WITH
26 DIFFERENT ALPHABETS

	a	b	c	d	e	f	g	h	i	j	k	l	m	n	o	p	q	r	s	t	u	v	w	x	y	z
1	B	C	D	E	F	G	H	I	J	K	L	M	N	O	P	Q	R	S	T	U	V	W	X	Y	Z	A
2	C	D	E	F	G	H	I	J	K	L	M	N	O	P	Q	R	S	T	U	V	W	X	Y	Z	A	B
3	D	E	F	G	H	I	J	K	L	M	N	O	P	Q	R	S	T	U	V	W	X	Y	Z	A	B	C
4	E	F	G	H	I	J	K	L	M	N	O	P	Q	R	S	T	U	V	W	X	Y	Z	A	B	C	D
5	F	G	H	I	J	K	L	M	N	O	P	Q	R	S	T	U	V	W	X	Y	Z	A	B	C	D	E
6	G	H	I	J	K	L	M	N	O	P	Q	R	S	T	U	V	W	X	Y	Z	A	B	C	D	E	F
7	H	I	J	K	L	M	N	O	P	Q	R	S	T	U	V	W	X	Y	Z	A	B	C	D	E	F	G
8	I	J	K	L	M	N	O	P	Q	R	S	T	U	V	W	X	Y	Z	A	B	C	D	E	F	G	H
9	J	K	L	M	N	O	P	Q	R	S	T	U	V	W	X	Y	Z	A	B	C	D	E	F	G	H	I
10	K	L	M	N	O	P	Q	R	S	T	U	V	W	X	Y	Z	A	B	C	D	E	F	G	H	I	J
11	L	M	N	O	P	Q	R	S	T	U	V	W	X	Y	Z	A	B	C	D	E	F	G	H	I	J	K
12	M	N	O	P	Q	R	S	T	U	V	W	X	Y	Z	A	B	C	D	E	F	G	H	I	J	K	L
13	N	O	P	Q	R	S	T	U	V	W	X	Y	Z	A	B	C	D	E	F	G	H	I	J	K	L	M
14	O	P	Q	R	S	T	U	V	W	X	Y	Z	A	B	C	D	E	F	G	H	I	J	K	L	M	N
15	P	Q	R	S	T	U	V	W	X	Y	Z	A	B	C	D	E	F	G	H	I	J	K	L	M	N	O
16	Q	R	S	T	U	V	W	X	Y	Z	A	B	C	D	E	F	G	H	I	J	K	L	M	N	O	P
17	R	S	T	U	V	W	X	Y	Z	A	B	C	D	E	F	G	H	I	J	K	L	M	N	O	P	Q
18	S	T	U	V	W	X	Y	Z	A	B	C	D	E	F	G	H	I	J	K	L	M	N	O	P	Q	R
19	T	U	V	W	X	Y	Z	A	B	C	D	E	F	G	H	I	J	K	L	M	N	O	P	Q	R	S
20	U	V	W	X	Y	Z	A	B	C	D	E	F	G	H	I	J	K	L	M	N	O	P	Q	R	S	T
21	V	W	X	Y	Z	A	B	C	D	E	F	G	H	I	J	K	L	M	N	O	P	Q	R	S	T	U
22	W	X	Y	Z	A	B	C	D	E	F	G	H	I	J	K	L	M	N	O	P	Q	R	S	T	U	V
23	X	Y	Z	A	B	C	D	E	F	G	H	I	J	K	L	M	N	O	P	Q	R	S	T	U	V	W
24	Y	Z	A	B	C	D	E	F	G	H	I	J	K	L	M	N	O	P	Q	R	S	T	U	V	W	X
25	Z	A	B	C	D	E	F	G	H	I	J	K	L	M	N	O	P	Q	R	S	T	U	V	W	X	Y
26	A	B	C	D	E	F	G	H	I	J	K	L	M	N	O	P	Q	R	S	T	U	V	W	X	Y	Z

Keyword: EARTH
               E A R T H E A R T H E A R T H E A R T H E
Plaintext: t h e e n e m y i n v a d e s a t d a w n
Ciphertext: X H V X U I M P B U X A U X Z E T U T D R

A dvance of the codes

Mary obviously didn't realize that there were far more sophisticated codes available to her at the time. Cryptography was becoming highly advanced, thanks to the progress made by generations of code makers.

The most famous of these was the Italian architect, Leon Battista Alberti (1404–72), who in the 1460s invented a form of substitution cipher using two separate cipher alphabets at the same time. In a five-letter word, for example, the first, third, and fifth letters would be enciphered using the first cipher alphabet, the second

different cipher alphabet on each numbered row, the first on row 1 starting with B, the second on row 2 with C, and so on to row 25 with Z, and finally, row 26 with A. The square is really a series of Caesar shifts, with the first row shifting one letter down the alphabet, the second two letters, and so on. This meant that each letter could be enciphered using a different row, and the order of the rows was determined by a keyword.

VIGENÈRE'S CIPHER WAS CRACKED BY INVENTOR CHARLES BABBAGE

and fourth letters using the second cipher alphabet.

T he square cipher

But why stop at only two cipher alphabets? Fifty years later, a French diplomat, Blaise de Vigenère (1523–96) took the obvious step and devised a 26-cipher code, which he set out in a square. Along the top of the square he wrote the plaintext alphabet a–z. Down the left he wrote the numbers 1–26. He then arranged a

T he keyword

This is where the Vigenère square becomes a very clever cipher. Take a word, such as EARTH, as your keyword, and write it out over and over again, EARTHEAREARTHEAR THEARTHEARTH. Then write the plaintext message underneath. The first letter of the message will then be enciphered using row 4, because the keyword starts with E, the second using row 26, which starts with A, and so on.

IN A SCENE FROM "THE MAN IN THE IRON
MASK" WITH LEONARDO DICAPRIO, THE
PRISONER IS THE KING'S TWIN BROTHER.

Because it is a five-letter
keyword, only five rows are
used. A longer keyword uses
more rows. As long as both
code maker and code breaker
share the same keyword, the
message can be enciphered and
deciphered with ease. No
keyword, big problem!

The man in the iron mask
Even harder to crack than the
Vigenère square was the
personal cipher of Louis XIV
of France (reigned 1643–1715).
His Great Cipher used different
numbers to represent every

possible sounding syllable. For
example, "enemy" has three
syllables. A code breaker was
therefore faced with hundreds
of meaningless numbers.

Louis' cipher remained secret
until 1890, when a French army
code breaker named Étienne
Bazeries finally cracked it. He
used frequency analysis to
discover which sets of numbers
represented the most common
French syllables.

One secret letter cast light on
a famous riddle. It concerned
the cowardice of a General
Vivien de Bulonde, who had
deserted his troops in a battle.
It read *"His majesty desires that you
immediately arrest General Bulonde*

…use him to be conducted to the fortress of Pignerole, where he will be locked in a cell under guard at night, and permitted to walk the battlements during the day under a mask."

A man wearing a mask, a prisoner of Louis XIV – ring any bells? Next time you see

…on the envelopes and copied the coded letters before resealing them and sending them on their way. Later in the day, outgoing diplomatic mail received the same treatment, with hundreds of letters a day being opened for inspection

THE BLACK CHAMBERS OPERATED WITHIN STRICT POSTAL TIMES

…that film with Leonardo diCaprio, remember that code breakers probably identified the real man in the iron mask more than 100 years ago!

The Black Chambers
By 1700, the rulers of Europe were organizing their code breakers into so-called Black Chambers. Here, foreign diplomatic letters were intercepted and any secrets they contained passed straight to the government. The most efficient of these chambers was in Vienna, capital of the powerful Austrian Hapsburg Empire. Diplomatic letters from around Europe addressed to embassies in Vienna were delivered to the Black Chamber at 7 a.m. Code breakers then melted the seals

and decoding. The intelligence gained was valuable to the Austrian emperors, but also profitable, as they often sold information to their allies.

THE VIENNESE BLACK CHAMBER SECRETLY OPENED AND RESEALED DIPLOMATIC MAIL WITHOUT AROUSING SUSPICIONS

THE CODE TALKERS

On July 26, 2001, five elderly Native Americans were presented with the Congressional Gold Medal – one of the United States' highest awards – by president George W. Bush. The five were the only survivors of a small group of men whose ability to speak a very rare language made them brilliant code makers. Together, they changed the course of World War II.

War breaks out

On December 7, 1941, Japanese planes attacked the US fleet at Pearl Harbor, Hawaii. The US now found itself at war in the Pacific Ocean, fighting the Japanese across thousands of square miles of sea and on hundreds of small islands.

At the time, all US military communications were enciphered through the SIGABA (or M-143-C) cipher machine. This machine was great at enciphering and deciphering messages, but it was very slow and inconvenient to use.

RECOGNITION OF THE NAVAJO'S HEROISM WAS SLOW IN COMING, BUT TODAY THEY ARE AMONG AMERICA'S MOST FAMOUS WAR HEROES.

The problem with SIGABA

First, the outgoing message had to be typed, letter by letter, into the machine and each enciphered letter then written down by hand, one by one.

Next, the complete enciphered message was passed to a radio operator, who transmitted it. At the other end, another radio operator received the message and again wrote it down by hand before passing it to a code operator who typed it into his own SIGABA machine to decipher it.

No place for a cipher

This complex procedure ensured that US secret codes remained unbroken by the Japanese. However, it required 30 minutes to encipher and decipher the message, space to set up all the equipment, and teams of radio transmitters and code operators to be stationed with each fighting unit.

On top of that, US troops often found themselves fighting in close combat with Japanese soldiers in hot jungle conditions. The troops had to be highly mobile and did not have the time nor space to use the cipher machine. Sending uncoded radio messages was also very dangerous. Some Japanese soldiers spoke English and could easily understand what the Americans were saying – even the slang words! The problem called for a radical and unusual solution.

WINDOW ROCK LIES AT THE HEART OF THE NAVAJO LANDS IN ARIZONA.

other European or Asian language – and is so complex that it is almost impossible for anyone else to understand.

Johnston, however, had learned their language and realized that if it could not be understood by his fellow Americans, it would never be understood by the Japanese!

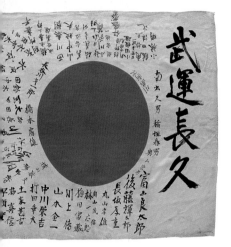

MANY JAPANESE SOLDIERS PREFERRED TO DIE RATHER THAN BE CAPTURED. SOME TIED PRAYER FLAGS LIKE THIS ONE TO THEIR HEADS DURING BATTLE.

The new recruits

Johnston suggested that pairs of Navajo men work as radio operators with each fighting battalion, sending and receiving messages in their own Navajo language.

The US government jumped at the idea, for the Navajo were one of the few tribes whose language had never been studied by scholars and was therefore totally unknown

The chosen tribe

The man who solved this problem was Philip Johnston, an engineer. He lived in Los Angeles, but as a child had grown up on the Navajo

AT FIRST, US SOLDIERS THOUGHT NAVAJO CODE WAS JAPANESE!

reservation in Arizona. The Navajos were a once-warlike tribe of Native Americans who had been settled by the US government in the 1860s on a vast reservation, where they farmed and kept animals. The Navajo language is unique to them – it has no links with any

outside the reservation. Within four months of Pearl Harbor, 29 Navajos began an eight-week training course with the US Marines.

What's Navajo for bomb?

At this point, a problem arose. The Navajo had lots of words

LOG ON...
www.history.navy.mil/
faqs/faq61-4.htm

for things they knew about and saw, such as birds and fish, but no words for things they had never experienced, such as fighter planes or submarines. So they drew up a list of 274 such words and gave them Navajo alternatives. Boats had fish names and planes had bird names. Bombs became "eggs," mortars (cannons) were "guns that squat," and an army squad was a "black sheep."

names of countries. America became known as "our mother," Britain as "between waters," Germany as "iron hat," and even Spain as "sheep pain!" For names of people and places, they used an

T he vocabulary grows
Soon, another 234 words were added to the list, including the

TWO NAVAJO CODE TALKERS OPERATE IN DENSE JUNGLE, CLOSE TO THE ENEMY.

alphabet of words for each letter. Thus Tokyo, the capital of Japan, became "Turkey, Owl,

Kid, Yucca, Owl," or *"Than-zie, ne-ahs-jsh, klizzie-yazzi, tsah-as-zih, ne-ahs-jsh"* in Navajo.

To avoid repetition of common letters, such as e, t, a, o, i, and n – which might have given Japanese code breakers vital clues to crack the code – extra words were used as alternatives. The second "o" in Tokyo could therefore become

"oil" (*"a-kha"*) or "onion" (*"tlo-chin"*).

The language barrier

The system had a false start, however, when US signal operators did not realize they had Navajo working alongside them. They thought the Japanese were broadcasting on the US army's wavelength!

But soon the use of Navajo code talking worked like a dream. What once took 30 minutes now took 20 seconds. US Navy Intelligence could not understand a word of what they said. Neither could the Japanese, who would have been amazed to discover that their airwaves were full of iron fish (submarines), hummingbirds (fighter planes),

THIS MEMORIAL IN WASHINGTON D.C. COMMEMORATES THE BATTLE OF IWO JIMA.

THE NAVAJO CODE WORD FOR FIGHTER PLANE WAS "HUMMINGBIRD." THIS P-51 MUSTANG WAS ONE OF THE BEST US FIGHTER PLANES OF THE WAR.

and sharks (destroyers), or *da-he-tih-hi*, *besh-lo*, and *ca-lo*, in Navajo.

Victory on Iwo Jima

As the US troops advanced, island by island, across the Pacific toward Japan, the Navajo code talkers played an increasingly important role. In the first days of the vital battle in February and March 1945 to capture the island of Iwo Jima, south of Japan, about 800 Navajo messages were sent, all without error. More than 21,000 Japanese soldiers died on Iwo Jima, as did 6,000 US troops. It was one of the bloodiest battles of the war, and many believed the island would never have been captured without the Navajo code talkers. They gave the US a crucial advantage against a most determined enemy.

Belated thanks

After the war the Navajo were forbidden to talk about their role. Their code remained classified information and their heroism was quietly forgotten.

WEIRD WORLD

BEFORE THE WAR, NAVAJO CHILDREN WERE PUNISHED FOR SPEAKING THEIR LANGUAGE. ENGLISH TEACHERS USED TO WASH THE CHILDREN'S MOUTHS OUT WITH SOAP.

Gradually, however, they received the acclaim they deserved, and in 1982, the US government made August 14 National Navajo Code Talkers Day. But the greatest tribute to the Navajo is the fact that their code is one of the only codes in history that was never cracked.

CODED SIGNALS

To send a coded message from one person to another normally requires a connection between them. This might be a letter sent by mail, or a signal broadcast by radio. But if these physical connections do not exist, how will your message be carried? Over the centuries people have invented solutions to that problem using signals that included smoke, flags, barrels, and baskets.

Smoke signals

During the 19th century, Native American lookouts would warn the tribe of approaching enemies by sending up a sudden cloud of smoke. Rapid puffs of smoke meant that the enemy was well-armed and numerous. Smoke signals depended on good weather, but did mean that tribes could stay in touch

THIS PAINTING DEPICTS NATIVE AMERICANS USING A BLANKET TO SEPARATE EACH CLOUD OF SMOKE.

A SMOKE SIGNAL WAS QUICKER THAN SENDING A MESSENGER

without having to send a messenger over vast areas of plain and prairie.

Flagging it

It wasn't only on land that people needed to find ways of

signaling over a distance, but also at sea.

If you're a sailor, the easiest and quickest way to send a visual signal is to hoist a flag. Some flags represent individual letters of the alphabet, others

THIS SINGLE FLAG REPRESENTS
THE NUMBER TWO.

represent numbers. This means that long messages require lots of flags. To save time, single flags can be used to signal a specific message, such as "I require medical assistance," or, more alarmingly, "I am on fire and have dangerous cargo on board, so keep clear!"

Different combinations of flags, or their positions on different masts, alter the meanings.

No flagging!

At the Battle of Trafalgar in 1805, however, it took 31 flags for the English admiral Lord Nelson to instruct his sailors

QUICK ACTION MAY BE NEEDED IF YOU SEE
THIS FLAG. IT MEANS "YOU ARE RUNNING
INTO DANGER!"

that *"England expects that every man will do his duty."* If no one else obeyed, at least the flag officer on board the HMS *Victory* earned his wage that day, as "duty" did not appear in Nelson's flag dictionary and had to be flagged up using an older, different code.

International code

The use of flags at sea dates back to the naval battles between the Greeks and Persians in the 5th century BC, while the first specially made signal flag was designed for the English fleet in 1369. During the 17th and 18th centuries, the British Royal Navy introduced an agreed upon code for both alphabet and number flags. The various British naval systems were replaced with one system in 1812, but other countries had their own flag codes, and could not easily decode the flags of foreign powers.

It was not until 1900 that an

43

International Code of Signals was officially brought into common use. Today, the navies, merchant fleets, ferries, and fishing vessels of the world all signal with the same coded flag language.

Semaphore

A variation of signal flags are semaphore flags. These are held in each hand at different heights (a bit like the hands of a clock) for each letter of the alphabet. Although semaphore flags have largely been replaced by telephone and radio, they are still used as a quick means of sending messages at sea. Like all flag and light signals, however, the advantage of semaphore is that it does not require radio waves and cannot be overheard by an enemy.

THESE SEMAPHORE SIGNALS REPRESENT THE LETTERS D AND K.

Light signals

Armies and navies have always used various forms of light signals involving torches or lanterns. But few of these could ever be used for signaling during the daytime, for obvious reasons.

The ancient Persians, however, had the idea of sending messages using sunlight reflected from polished shields. This was an early version of the heliograph – a mirror mounted on a tripod, and aimed by using a sighting vain.

To be effective over long distances,

LOG ON...
inter.scoutnet.org/
semaphore/

the heliograph needed bright sunlight. A shutter on the mirror allowed messages to be sent in Morse code over a distance of up to 22 miles (35 km).

Before the arrival of radio, the heliograph was the British army's main transmission system for patrolling the vast frontiers of the British Empire. In the US, the army used it to counter the effectiveness of Native American smoke signals in the Midwestern states.

THE RAILWAYS STILL USE A FORM OF TWO-ARM SEMAPHORE. A RAISED ARM MEANS "ALL CLEAR AHEAD."

WEIRD WORLD
HELIOGRAPHS WERE EVENTUALLY REPLACED BY SIGNALING LAMPS THAT BURNED PURE LIME IN A CONTROLLED SUPPLY OF OXYGEN. THIS "LIMELIGHT" MADE THEM INTENSELY BRIGHT AND PERFECT FOR THE THEATER!

the Americans' prearranged signal, and their fellow revolutionaries a few miles away could easily read it. But the

A barrel of meaning
In certain desperate situations people have used improvised methods of communicating in code. Americans fighting for independence in the 1770s outwitted the British army redcoats by hoisting a barrel, a basket, and a flag up a post. The order and position of the items on the post spelled out

enemy had no idea what this coded signal meant, or that a large army was about to attack them!

In war, the strength of a code may be as important as the strength of an army.

SECRET NUMBERS

One of the most common forms of code is number code. Numbers are essential to our lives. They are used to record all kinds of data from pocket change to sports results. But numbers can also be used in place of letters to form codes that are extremely difficult to crack. Two number codes have become particularly famous. One promised treasure, the other led to war.

Buried treasure

In 1885, a short pamphlet was published in Lynchburg, Virginia. It contained *"authentic statements regarding the treasure buried in 1819 and 1821, near Buford, in Bedford County, Virginia, and which has never been recovered."* In it were three lengthy lists of numbers, the Beale ciphers.

The story behind this buried treasure is very strange, if it is in fact true. Allegedly, a Mr. Thomas Beale checked into a hotel in Lynchburg in January 1820 and left in the spring. He returned again in January 1822, this time entrusting a locked, iron box to the safekeeping of the manager, Robert Morriss. Later that year, Beale wrote to Morriss telling him that if no one returned within 10 years to claim the box, then Morriss was to open it.

BEALE LEFT THE CIPHERS IN A LOCKED BOX. HE WENT TO GREAT LENGTHS TO KEEP THE LOCATION OF THE GOLD SECRET.

No one returned in 1832 or 1842, so eventually, in 1845, Morriss opened the box. It contained a letter from Beale describing how he had buried large quantities of gold. It also contained three numerical ciphers – the first describing the treasure's location, the second its contents, and the third who was to receive a share. Morriss told all this to a friend, who, after Morriss's death, wrote down everything in the pamphlet.

M any numbers
Although we don't know the name of this friend, we do know

that he was an expert code breaker. He realized that the numbers in each cipher represented letters of the alphabet, but that each letter was represented by many different numbers. The second cipher, for example, had

LOG ON...
www.unmuseum.org/
bealhtm

THE TREASURE MAY BE BURIED SOMEWHERE IN THESE HILLS IN VIRGINIA.

WEIRD WORLD
GEORGE AND CLAYTON HART DEVOTED THEIR LIVES TO BREAKING THE TWO UNREAD BEALE CIPHERS. ONCE, THEY THOUGHT THEY'D LOCATED THE GOLD AND USED DYNAMITE TO EXCAVATE THE SITE. THEY FOUND NOTHING.

more than 750 numbers, ranged from 2 to 1,005 and repeated many numbers. Our man guessed that the key to these ciphers was a book, or a long piece of text.

Independent thinking

This was no easy task. After checking hundreds of books and writings, he discovered that the Declaration of Independence – one of the most famous texts in American history – was the key to the second cipher. It starts "115, 73, 24." The 115th word of the Declaration starts with I, the 73rd with H, the 24th with A, and so on. Put it all together, and the deciphered text reveals "I have deposited about four miles from Buford, in an excavation or vault, six feet below the surface of the ground...gold and silver packed into iron pots with iron covers."

THE DECLARATION OF INDEPENDENCE UNLOCKED THE SECOND CIPHER. BUT WHICH TEXTS WERE USED TO ENCIPHER THE FIRST AND THIRD?

Choose a book

Book ciphers are very clever. Take a well-known piece of writing, such as the Lord's Prayer or the first page of *Harry Potter*, and number each word. Number 1 now represents the first letter of the first word, 2 the first letter of the second word, and so on. All our man had to do was identify the book that was used and the Beale cipher would be broken!

Treasure hunters soon descended on the small village of Buford and dug around in a radius of four miles. But to this day, no treasure has ever been found, and no one has yet discovered the texts to unlock the other two ciphers. Could it all be a hoax or a case of skillful encipherment? No one knows.

NO ONE KNOWS WHETHER BEALE'S GOLD IS IN THE FORM OF BARS, INGOTS, GRAIN, OR NUGGETS – IF IT EXISTS AT ALL!

The Zimmermann telegram

In 1914, World War I broke out in Europe. The US remained neutral and refused to support either side, but in January 1917 Germany changed its tactics in order to force its main enemy, Britain, to surrender. It decided to start a submarine war against all ships, including American ships, that were supplying Britain with food. The Germans hoped to starve Britain out of the war. They knew that this might provoke the US into declaring war against Germany, so they came up with a daring backup plan.

The German foreign secretary, Arthur Zimmermann (1864–1940) wanted to urge Mexico to invade the US and reclaim those states, such as Arizona and Texas, that it had lost to the US in the 19th century. He hoped this attack would keep the US out of the war in Europe. Zimmermann sent a telegram to the German ambassador in Washington for onward transmission to Mexico, to inform the Mexican government of the plan.

> ### WEIRD WORLD
> THE HEAD OF BRITISH INTELLIGENCE, ADMIRAL HALL, DISTRACTED ATTENTION FROM HIS CODE BREAKTHROUGH BY PLANTING A STORY IN THE PRESS CRITICIZING THE FAILURE OF BRITISH INTELLIGENCE TO DECODE THE TELEGRAM!

The secret agent

The telegram, which consisted of a long list of numbers, three, four, or five digits long, was intercepted by the British and sent to Room 40 in the

THE GERMANS WANTED MEXICO TO RECLAIM TEXAS, ARIZONA, AND NEW MEXICO FROM THE UNITED STATES.

Admiralty, the nerve center of British intelligence. There, the code breakers deciphered it and immediately realized its

decision that turned a European war into a world war and led to the surrender of Germany on November 11, 1918.

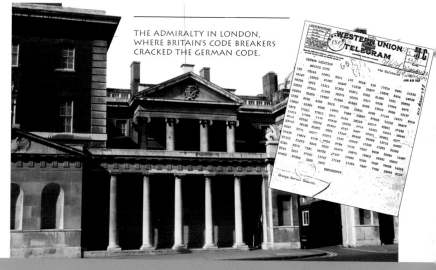

THE ADMIRALTY IN LONDON, WHERE BRITAIN'S CODE BREAKERS CRACKED THE GERMAN CODE.

THE GERMANS NEVER REALIZED THEIR CODE HAD BEEN BROKEN

importance. However, they did not want the Germans to know that the code had been broken, in case Germany then developed a stronger code. So they assigned a British secret agent in Mexico City to obtain a deciphered copy of the telegram by infiltrating the Mexican telegraph office.

In February 1917, the telegram was released to the US press and the public was shocked. On April 2, the US declared war on Germany, a

The Germans thought the deciphered telegram had been stolen from the Mexican government. Only in the mid-1920s did they discover that all their wartime codes had been cracked and read by the British. They were so horrified when they found out that they were determined to have the most sophisticated cipher machine technology could provide. And that, as we shall see, proved far more difficult for the British to crack.

CODE MACHINES

Every code described so far has been invented or cracked by sheer brain power. Using your head to break codes can be very hard work and take a lot of concentration. Machines, however, can do what humans do quicker and often better. Over the years, a range of machines has been devised to make and break codes. The first were simple revolving discs. The most recent is the computer.

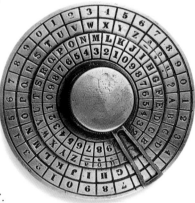

THE LETTERS AND NUMBERS ON THE OUTER CIRCLE OF THIS CIPHER DISC CAN BE ALIGNED WITH DIFFERENT LETTERS AND NUMBERS ON THE INNER CIRCLE.

A two-wheel spin

The first cipher machine was invented by Leon Alberti, the 15th-century Italian architect we met some pages back. He made two copper discs, one larger than the other, wrote the alphabet around the edge of each one, and then attached them together with a pin so that each could rotate separately. Line up the letter A on the outer disc with A on the inner disc and then move the inner disc one or more letters to obtain a cipher alphabet. This was a type of mechanical Caesar shift.

Similar devices were used to encode messages during the

THIS CIPHER DEVICE IS SIMILAR TO THOMAS JEFFERSON'S. EACH DISC IS DETACHABLE AND CAN BE ARRANGED IN ANY ORDER.

LOG ON…
www.bsa.scouting.org/
fun/morse/index.html

Civil War (1861–65). The "Code-o-Graph" – again based on the same idea but with numbers rather than letters – was used by Captain Midnight in his popular 1930s US radio show. Fans could even write in for one!

Spin doctors

A device invented first by an American, Decius Wadsworth, in 1817 and then again by the British scientist, Sir Charles Wheatstone, in 1867 was even

(remember him – the one who cracked "the man in the iron mask" letter?). Bazeries came up with a cylindrical cipher device in 1891. But almost 100 years before him, Thomas Jefferson (1743–1826), leading author of the US Declaration of Independence, onetime president of the United States, inventor, and genius, came up

JEFFERSON WAS TOO BUSY EVER TO USE HIS OWN WHEEL-CIPHER!

more complex. Both of these also had two discs, but with a gearing mechanism that spun them in a random way.

A 25-wheel spin

Far more brilliant than any of these was another device with two separate inventors. The less famous one was the French code breaker, Étienne Bazeries

with a similar device.

Their wheel-cipher machines consisted of about 25 numbered discs – each one bearing the letters of the alphabet in a different random order. The discs rotated around a central shaft. To encipher a message, the code maker arranged the discs in a set numerical order (2, 15, 19, etc).

He then spun them so that the first 25 letters of his plaintext message could be read along one row of discs. He then read 25 letters off any other row and this became his ciphertext. This process was repeated until the message was entirely enciphered.

To decipher the message, a cryptanalyst set up the first 25 letters of the enciphered message and then looked for the row bearing the plaintext. He repeated this until the full message was revealed.

These rotating discs were a major step forward in code-making history. Their

most famous code machine, however, was anything but secret. On May 24, 1844, Samuel Morse (1791–1872) sent a message from Washington D.C. to Baltimore. The famous message was simple – *"What hath God wrought"* – but the technology was revolutionary.

THIS FAMOUS MORSE CODE SIGNAL SPELLS "S.O.S." ("SAVE OUR SOULS") AND IS SENT BY VESSELS IN DISTRESS.

Morse had strung up a 37-mile (60-km) wire between the two cities and then sent pulses of electrical current down the wire. Using a simple on-off switch, he broke this current up

> ## WEIRD WORLD
> THE OFFICIAL INTERNATIONAL MORSE CODE DISTRESS SIGNAL S.O.S. WAS FIRST TRANSMITTED AT SEA FROM THE *TITANIC*, 65 MINUTES AFTER SHE HIT THE ICEBERG AND 95 MINUTES BEFORE SHE SANK.

importance became clear when code breakers tried to crack the Enigma machine, as we shall see in the next chapter.

Morse code

All of these machines were devised to create and break secret codes and ciphers. The

into short and long pulses, or dots and dashes. Each different combination of dots and dashes represented one letter of the alphabet or a number from 0 to 9 – one dot and one dash represented A, two dashes followed by two dots represented Z.

MORSE CODE WAS TRANSMITTED BY A TAPPING DEVICE LIKE THIS ONE. A MORSE MESSAGE WAS RECEIVED ON A GROOVED STRIP OF PAPER PRINTED FROM A RECEIVER.

The name of this invention

was the telegraph, and it soon connected people and countries as never before. The code used to transmit messages became known as Morse code. Since its introduction, the dots and dashes of Morse code have been used to send messages around the world via the telegraph wire, signal lamp, and radio waves, to broadcast signals from ships in distress, and to catch criminals. During World War II, more than 40 million words a year were transmitted in Morse from one radio station in Britain alone. Some code!

THE TITANIC RECEIVED NINE MORSE CODE MESSAGES WARNING OF ICE. DESPITE THIS, THE CAPTAIN BELIEVED THE SHIP WAS IN NO DANGER.

CRACKING ENIGMA

By the start of the World World II, cipher machines had been invented that made all earlier versions obsolete. The Purple machine was allowing Japan to dominate the Pacific, and in Germany the Nazis had Enigma – a cipher so unbreakable that for a long time Hitler was winning his war in Europe. It took some of the most brilliant minds in the world to crack Enigma, and their achievement heralded the computer age.

The Purple machine

Shortly before the outbreak of war in the Pacific, the Japanese invented a cipher machine of breathtaking complexity. Known as "Purple" by the US, it operated with an intricate telephone wiring system and a key-in plugboard that allowed for millions of cipher combinations. To encipher a message, a chosen key was set, and the plaintext entered on the keyboard of an electric typewriter. The message then passed through the maze of wiring, and the coded message printed out

THE ATTACK ON PEARL HARBOR CAME EARLY ON A SUNDAY MORNING WHEN MANY SERVICEMEN WERE OFF DUTY.

on a second electric typewriter. The Japanese were confident that Purple was unbreakable, but the US was able to break it. By September 1940, a team of US code breakers led by William Friedman were deciphering Purple messages after building a replica of the machine.

P earl Harbor warning

Deciphered Purple messages warned of a Japanese attack in December 1941 but did not name the hour or the place. As a result, the US was caught unawares when the devastating surprise raid took place at Pearl Harbor in Hawaii. The attack killed 2,300 Americans, and the US was drawn into World War II.

THE PURPLE MACHINE DIFFERED FROM ENIGMA BY HAVING TELEPHONE SWITCHES RATHER THAN ROTATING SCRAMBLERS.

who built the first model as early as 1918. Enigma was hugely complex. It had three main parts – a keyboard to type in the plaintext letters, a scrambling unit to turn those

DECODED INFORMATION FROM PURPLE WAS KNOWN AS "MAGIC"

E nigma

Friedman's Purple replica was an amazing engineering achievement. But it seemed primitive compared with the invention needed to crack the cipher used by the Nazis.

The Nazis' Enigma machine was the brainchild of a German inventor, Arthur Scherbius,

letters into ciphertext, and an illuminated lampboard to show the enciphered letters. The scrambling unit consisted of three, interchangeable, rotating scramblers. Below the keyboard was a plugboard containing six cables. Enigma looked like some weird typewriter stuffed into a small wooden box.

The machine provided a level of secrecy greater than anything in the history of ciphers. And it was perfect for Hitler, who needed to keep his invasion plans secret from the rest of Europe. Thanks to Enigma, he had the most secure cipher system in the world.

How it worked

The operator placed the three scramblers into the machine in a certain order, say 1–3–2 or 3–1–2, and set the scramblers by rotating them. For example, E on the first scrambler lined up with H on the second and W on the third. Finally, he arranged the plugboard cables. These allowed him to encipher a message even further by swapping six pairs of letters on the keyboard,

so that B swapped with G, V with J, and so on, six times. Enigma was then ready to use.

The operator then typed in the first letter of the message. An electrical current passed from the keyboard through the plugboard and the three scramblers. The current then returned via a different route to the lampboard, where it lit up a bulb to indicate the enciphered letter. When the entire message had been enciphered and written down, it was transmitted by radio using Morse code.

At the other end, the receiver wrote down the enciphered message. He arranged the rotor setting on his Enigma machine so that it was exactly the same as the operator's and keyed in the message. Like a mirror, the plugboard and scramblers reversed the process and, letter by letter, the deciphered message lit up on the lampboard.

Enigma variations

As if this weren't complicated enough, the three scramblers revolved at different speeds after each letter was typed in. They only returned to their

EACH MONTH, THE GERMANS ISSUED A NEW CODE BOOK LISTING THE DAY'S CIPHER SETTINGS FOR ENIGMA.

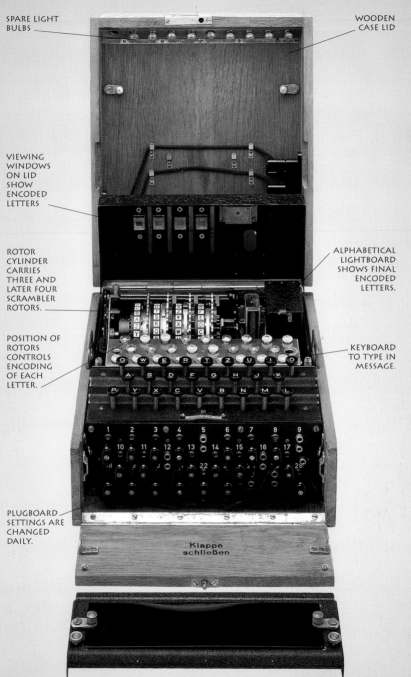

SPARE LIGHT BULBS

WOODEN CASE LID

VIEWING WINDOWS ON LID SHOW ENCODED LETTERS

ROTOR CYLINDER CARRIES THREE AND LATER FOUR SCRAMBLER ROTORS.

ALPHABETICAL LIGHTBOARD SHOWS FINAL ENCODED LETTERS.

POSITION OF ROTORS CONTROLS ENCODING OF EACH LETTER.

KEYBOARD TO TYPE IN MESSAGE.

PLUGBOARD SETTINGS ARE CHANGED DAILY.

Klappe schließen

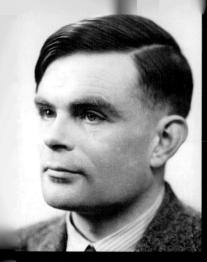

ALAN TURING BUILT COMPUTERS TO CRACK ENIGMA. BECAUSE HIS WORK WAS SECRET, HIS AMAZING ACHIEVEMENT WAS NEVER ACKNOWLEDGED IN HIS LIFETIME.

original settings after about 17,000 letters. Each scrambler could also be set in 26 different orientations – one for each letter of the alphabet – and placed in six different orders. Multiply the 17,576 orientations (26 x 26 x 26) with the six orders and the staggering 100,391,791,500 ways to pair the six plugboard cables and you get a possible 10,000,000,000,000,000 different Enigma settings!

Breaking the code
Polish intelligence was the first to try and crack Enigma. As a neighbor of Nazi Germany, Poland feared for its existence. The Poles gave the job to their best code breaker – a 23-year-old mathematician called Marian Rejewski. His first problem was that the Enigma cipher changed daily. The Nazis issued a new code book each month stating which day key to use. That meant which plugboard setting, scrambler arrangement, and scrambler orientation to make each day. For even more security, the Nazis only used the day key to transmit a three-letter message key, keyed in twice, to create a unique cipher for each message.

Repeat success
Rejewski knew that each message started with the repeated three-letter message key. From this, he managed to

work out a complete enciphered alphabet using the pairs of repeated letters of the message key. He then built six machines, which he called "bombes," one for each possible scrambler arrangement, to find the day key. He was soon able to read most German messages.

Rejewski's achievement was immense. He had proved that Enigma could be broken. However, the Nazis soon increased the number of scramblers to five and the number of plugboard cables from six to ten. The number of possible day keys now grew to 159,000,000,000,000,000,000!

As the Poles prepared for a German invasion in 1939 they handed over blueprints for the

WEIRD WORLD

REJEWSKI'S BOMBES GOT THEIR NAME EITHER BECAUSE OF THE TICKING NOISE THEY MADE OR BECAUSE HE GOT HIS INSPIRATION WHILE EATING AN ICE CREAM KNOWN AS A BOMBE!

bombes to the British, who were stunned by the Polish achievement.

Bletchley Park
The British government's code breaking center was based in

THIS SCENE FROM THE MOVIE "U-571" SHOWS US SEAMEN BOARDING A U-BOAT TO CAPTURE THE ENIGMA CODE BOOK. IN REALITY, THE BRITISH CAPTURED IT.

Bletchley Park, a stately home in Buckinghamshire, England. Here, a bizarre assortment of mathematicians, scientists, linguists, chess champions, an expert on porcelain, and other brainy people were recruited to crack Enigma.

The man who won the war

Bletchley's most brilliant recruit was Alan Turing, a young mathematician from Cambridge University. Turing made two major discoveries. First, that Enigma had a weakness – it couldn't encipher any letter as itself. A couldn't be A. It always

letters stood for – it was the *wetter* (weather) report!

From this, Turing identified the Enigma settings that turned *wetter* into ciphertext. He found that there was a loop connecting plaintext and ciphertext letters: w–E, e–T, t–W, for example. He then built a vast bombe, far bigger than Rejewski's, and ran the loop through it. As each loop established itself, the electrical circuit became complete and

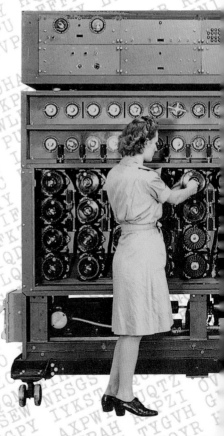

WEIRD WORLD

BLETCHLEY PARK RECRUITED SOME CODE BREAKERS BY ASKING READERS OF THE *TELEGRAPH* NEWSPAPER TO COMPLETE THE CROSSWORD PUZZLE IN UNDER 12 MINUTES. THOSE WHO REPLIED WERE INVITED TO COMPLETE ANOTHER SPECIAL CROSSWORD TEST.

had to be a different letter. This gave him an important crib (clue) for cracking the cipher. Secondly, he realized that many German messages were very similar. One message sent at 6.05 a.m. every morning featured a six-letter ciphertext. He figured out what these six

the bombe simply stopped.

By early 1942, 16 bombes worked day and night to decipher Enigma. Within an hour, all that day's messages could be deciphered.

Secrets of the submarine

One of the problems Turing faced was that there were different versions of Enigma. The German army used a day key that was different from the navy's, which had its own advanced form of Enigma machine. Naval operators were careful not to send typical messages, like the daily *wetter* report, that might give clues to a code breaker.

In October 1942, British sailors boarded crippled submarine U-559 in the eastern Mediterranean and rescued the code books for Naval Enigma. Bletchley Park could now read all naval messages in the North Atlantic. This was at a time when U-boats were sinking dozens of vital supply ships each month in an attempt to starve Britain into surrender.

The computer age

The success of Turing's bombes in decoding Enigma messages helped the Allies defeat the Nazis on every front. Most importantly, they revealed a detailed picture of German troop positions in France before D-Day, June 6, 1944. The bombes put an end to the cipher machine as a means of encryption. The computer age had begun.

TURING'S BOMBES (BELOW) WERE THE SIZE OF WARDROBES, BUT HIS NEXT CREATION WAS EVEN LARGER – COLOSSUS, THE FIRST TRUE ELECTRICAL COMPUTER.

LOG ON...
www.bletchleypark.org.uk

COMPUTER CODES

Many people have computers at home – this book was written on one. But how many of us know how they really work? Not just the on/off switch, the keyboard, and all those chips inside. Rather, how does a computer compute? How does it think? The answer is that it does so in code, and where there is a computer code there are always computer hackers.

Coded bits

Computers don't use the letters or numbers we're familiar with. They talk in a coded language known as binary code. Binary consists of two digits, 0 and 1, known as bits. These are used instead of our usual decimal 1000001), lowercase letters (a = 1100001), punctuation marks (! = 0100001), symbols (&= 0100110), and so on.

Babbage's engines

You might think computers are a recent invention, but in fact

THE FIRST COMPUTER WAS BUILT NEARLY 200 YEARS AGO

system – 10 digits of 0 to 9 – because it's easier for computers to work with multiples of 2 digits than it is with multiples of 10.

To convert letters into binary code, computers use a standard system that gives a seven-digit binary number to every key you find on a computer keyboard – capitals (A =

they're coming up to their 200th birthday! The first computer – Difference Engine No. 1, as it was known – was devised in 1823 by the English inventor and enthusiastic code breaker, Charles Babbage.

THIS RECONSTRUCTION OF DIFFERENCE ENGINE NO. 2 IS IN LONDON'S SCIENCE MUSEUM. THE PRINCIPLES BEHIND IT ARE THE SAME AS THE MODERN COMPUTER.

It was designed to make complex calculations, had 25,000 parts, and cost £17,470 (about $84,000) – a staggering sum in the 1820s!

Colossus
The real advance came in 1937. Alan Turing – the brilliant mathematician who went on to crack Enigma – wrote a famous scientific paper that described a machine programmed to answer any question that could be answered logically. He called it the "Universal Turing Machine." Six years later, World War II brought his

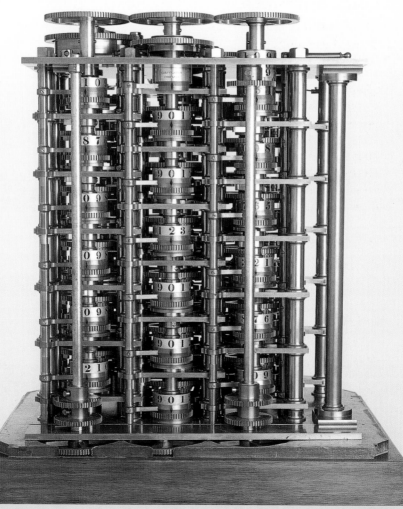

ALTHOUGH COLOSSUS WAS DESIGNED SOLELY FOR CODE BREAKING, IT WAS THE FIRST ELECTRONIC COMPUTER OF ITS KIND, AND A MARVEL OF THE AGE.

colleagues, Max Newman, invented a machine based on the Universal Turing Machine that could. It was called Colossus, because it was enormous. It had 1,500 electronic valves that could process data fed to it by hole-punched tape. The importance of Colossus is that it could be programmed, just like a modern computer.

machine to life. In addition to Enigma, the Nazis had an even more secure cipher machine called Lorenz. This was used to encipher the most secret messages between German generals and Hitler himself. Turing's machines (bombes) were too slow to decipher Lorenz messages, so one of his

MODERN COMPUTERS STORE THEIR CODES ON MINISCULE SILICON MICROCHIPS.

Silicon chips

Unfortunately, Colossus was classified as top secret, so when the war ended in 1945, Colossus was destroyed and its blueprints burned. For years afterward, everyone thought that the first true computer was the Electronic Numerical Integrator And Calculator – ENIAC for short – which was built at the University of

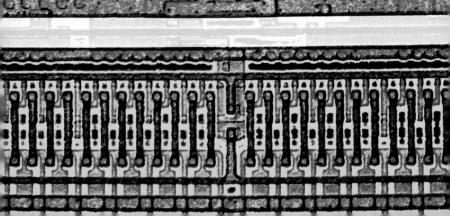

Pennsylvania in 1945.
It had 18,000 electronic valves,
and could make 5,000
calculations per second.
From ENIAC came all
modern computers.

In 1959, the first electronic
circuit printed entirely on
silicon was invented.
Computers then rapidly shrank
in size and cost, with the
world's first personal computer
appearing in 1975.

The power of Lucifer

Today, every government,
army, and business uses
computers for everything from
aiming missiles to conducting
massive business deals.
Millions of individuals give
out credit card and other
personal details over the
internet to obtain CDs, books,
and other items. Much of this
vast flow of information has to

be kept secret, and so must be
sent in code.

Since the 1960s, code makers
have been inventing codes to
make business communications
safer. One of the most famous,
and the most secure, is Lucifer.

WEIRD WORLD

COMPUTER CODE MAKERS USE
THREE FICTIONAL PEOPLE WHEN
DISCUSSING COMPLEX ISSUES SUCH
AS PUBLIC KEY ENCRYPTION.
THEIR NAMES ARE ALICE, BOB,
AND EVE!

Lucifer is now the official
standard encryption code in the
US. It translates messages into
binary digits and then shuffles
those digits like a pack of
cards. The process is repeated
until the message is completely
mixed up, and is then ready to

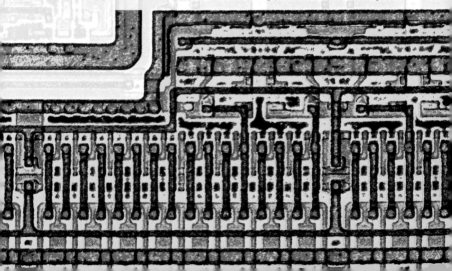

send. The receiver reverses the process to decipher the message.

Lucifer was so safe that the US government's National Security Agency couldn't decipher the messages of criminals. They demanded that

its keys be simplified for security reasons.

The weakness of keys

Keys have always been needed to encipher or decipher a message. Remember our five-letter keyword to unlock the Vigenère cipher? But keys have also been the main weakness of ciphers. Sender and receiver

LUCIFER DIVIDES A MESSAGE INTO 64 BINARY BLOCKS (BELOW). IT THEN SHUFFLES AND SPLITS THEM INTO BLOCKS OF 32.

both needed an identical key to lock and unlock a coded message. If a general wanted to send a coded message to his troops, how could he deliver the key to them without the risk of an enemy capturing it? This was the problem with Enigma. Sender and receiver both used identical keys set down in a monthly code book. If a code book was captured, the Allies could quickly decode all the month's messages.

held by you alone, for you to decipher the email. The problem of how to send an identical key safely therefore doesn't arise.

Code makers made this breakthrough by inventing a cipher that uses a one-way mathematical sum. In other words, a sum that's easy to do, but almost impossible to undo

LOG ON...
www.museums.reading.
ac.uk/vmoc/babbage/

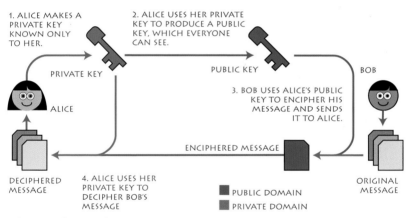

1. ALICE MAKES A PRIVATE KEY KNOWN ONLY TO HER.

2. ALICE USES HER PRIVATE KEY TO PRODUCE A PUBLIC KEY, WHICH EVERYONE CAN SEE.

PRIVATE KEY

PUBLIC KEY

BOB

ALICE

3. BOB USES ALICE'S PUBLIC KEY TO ENCIPHER HIS MESSAGE AND SENDS IT TO ALICE.

ENCIPHERED MESSAGE

DECIPHERED MESSAGE

4. ALICE USES HER PRIVATE KEY TO DECIPHER BOB'S MESSAGE

■ PUBLIC DOMAIN
■ PRIVATE DOMAIN

ORIGINAL MESSAGE

PUBLIC KEY ENCRYPTION

A new kind of key

There seemed to be no way around this key problem until the 1970s, when computers and mathematics provided the answer – sender and receiver needn't have identical keys! Instead, you have one "public key" for anyone to send you an enciphered message via email, and one secret and private key,

unless you've got the formula. The sum uses prime numbers, that is, numbers such as 3, 5, and so on, that can only be divided by themselves and 1. Your software chooses two very large prime numbers for you and keeps them secret. This is your private key. It then multiplies them together to make a huge number. This will be your public key, which you can make available to all, like a phone number. Anyone can then send you a coded message using your public key. However, no one except you can decipher it, because only you know which prime numbers make up your private key – the primes needed to unlock the big number. If your prime numbers are large enough, it's almost impossible to find out what they are. The most powerful computers in the world would take billions of years to work it out.

Hackers' heaven

Such complex keys and ciphers are, however, red flags to those bulls known as hackers. A hacker is someone who hacks or breaks into a computer

system, either by cracking a code or finding a way around one. Some hack in to steal and sell commercial secrets. Others hack in for political reasons and wreck the website of a corporation they don't like.

Some hackers, however, hack in just because they can. Each computer code, no matter how complex, challenges a hacker to break it or avoid it.

WEIRD WORLD
IN MAY 2000, A VIRUS CORRUPTED MILLIONS OF COMPUTERS IN A MATTER OF HOURS. IT SPREAD ITSELF VIA AN EMAIL ENTITLED "ILoveYou." MOST PEOPLE COULD NOT RESIST OPENING IT, THEREBY RELEASING THE VIRUS!

Once they get past the code, some hackers alter people's databases, causing massive damage as they delete files or make secret information public. Others go even further and invent computer viruses – complicated codes that once downloaded corrupt computers and destroy data. Viruses with names such as Bouncing Ball, Melissa, and Love Bug have caused havoc around the world.

In May 2001, the website of Steve Gibson, a US computer security expert, was bombarded with millions of requests for information, causing it to crash. The requests all came from a 13-year old hacker in Wisconsin, who called himself "Wicked." Wicked is not alone. There are thousands of hackers worldwide who, like Wicked, love testing their skills against the code makers of government and big business.

HACKERS ARE SKILLED AT COVERING THEIR TRACKS AND CAN BE HARD TO TRACE. MOST HACKERS ARE TEENAGED BOYS.

THE GREATEST CODE OF ALL

All the codes we have seen so far have been devised by humans, using pen and paper, cipher machines, or computers. But the most complex code of all is the natural genetic code inside our own bodies. This code is the building plan for all human life. It makes each one of us unique. Decoding it is one of our greatest scientific achievements.

The genetic code

To make sense of this mind-bogglingly complex code, we need to understand a few facts about ourselves. Our bodies are made up of cells – about 50,000 trillion of them, give or take a few. Inside each cell is a nucleus, and inside each nucleus there are 23 pairs of chromosomes. A chromosome contains a single, scrunched-up molecule of deoxyribonucleic acid – DNA for short. Although a DNA molecule is only billionths of a millimeter thick, if it were stretched out, it would be 6 ft

THIS CROSS-SECTION OF A SINGLE CELL SHOWS THE NUCLEUS IN PINK, WHERE ALL THE CHROMOSOMES ARE TO BE FOUND.

THE TIGHTLY COILED DNA MOLECULE SCRUNCHES UP INSIDE A CHROMOSOME.

(2 m) long! It's made up of two slender strands that spiral around each other and that are held together by pairs of chemicals, known as bases, just as the rungs of a ladder hold it together. There are four bases, called adenine (A), thymine (T), guanine (G), and cytosine (C). A only ever pairs with T, and G always pairs with C, making four possible pairs – AT, TA, GC, CG.

WEIRD WORLD
THE DNA OF EVERY CREATURE IN THE WORLD IS SIMILAR. THIS MAY BE BECAUSE WE ALL EVOLVED FROM THE EARTH'S VERY EARLIEST LIFE-FORM – BACTERIA!

contain a complete set of plans for building the human body. The DNA in each chromosome holds the instructions, or genes, that control the way a particular cell works. So the red cells in your blood receive instructions that are different from those given to the cells in your hair or your lungs.

I t's all in your genes
Together, the 23 pairs of chromosomes inside each cell

P rotein control
DNA gives these instructions by telling the cell to make proteins. The proteins are crucial because they're in charge of all the chemical changes taking place inside the body. By producing proteins, therefore, DNA controls the way a cell works and therefore the way the body works.

THIS ULTRASOUND SCAN (ABOVE) SHOWS TWINS IN THE WOMB. IDENTICAL TWINS SHARE THE SAME GENES,

UNLESS YOU'RE A TWIN, YOUR GENES MAKE YOU UNIQUE. EVEN FINGERPRINTS ARE NEVER THE SAME.

What you inherit

So why all this advanced biology? Because those all-important genes are not only responsible for how your body works but also, when they break down or go wrong, which illnesses you might get. Genes are also passed down (inherited) from parent to child in a process known as heredity. So if both your parents have blue eyes, so might you. This is illnesses, such as diabetes, are also hereditary, and can be passed down through the generations.

The genetic code is the key

DNA MOLECULES HOLD THE CODE FOR BUILDING A WHOLE BODY

because the genes you inherited from your parents have given instructions to the cells in your eyes to be blue, not brown. Some 4,000

to knowing everything about our bodies. The only problem was that, until recently, no one could decipher the code.

The double helix

In fact, until quite recently, no one was sure where in the body the genetic code was stored or what it looked like. The idea of heredity was only worked out in 1865, and chromosomes were only discovered in 1882.

GENES PASS FROM PARENTS TO CHILDREN, SO WE MAY LOOK LIKE MOM OR DAD, OR BOTH, AS WELL AS HAVING A UNIQUE LOOK OF OUR OWN.

Scientists had a long way to go before breaking this particular code. They made a good start in 1952, when the English physicist Rosalind Franklin proved that DNA molecules were spiral in shape. She did this by turning strands of DNA into crystal and firing X-rays through it, creating a pattern that she could study.

LOG ON...
www.ornl.gov/hgmis/

THIS MODEL OF A DOUBLE HELIX SHOWS HOW PAIRS OF BASES (A AND T, C AND G) ONLY EVER PAIR WITH THE SAME PARTNER.

The breakthrough

The next year, an American, James Watson and a Briton, Francis Crick, who both worked at Cambridge University, England, made the big breakthrough. Using Franklin's evidence, they discovered that DNA consisted of not one but two spirals held together by chemical bases (the "rungs" of the ladder described earlier). They called this odd shape a double helix. For their work, the pair shared the Nobel Prize for medicine in 1962.

Mapping the genome

In 1990, scientists began the massive task of determining the order of all the genes inside human chromosomes. The aim was to map the entire human genome, or genetic makeup of the body, in order to understand how it worked and what every gene did. As part of their research, they cut a small fragment of DNA out of a chromosome. After some clever chemical processing, they analyzed the fragments with lasers to find out where in the chromosome the fragment came. Fragment by fragment, computers

THE FIRST CREATURE TO HAVE ITS GENOME DECODED WAS THIS SIMPLE WORM.

built up a complete picture of the genes in each chromosome.

Epic task

The scientists' task was immense. They assumed that humans possessed about 100,000 different genes in each cell, and that each gene had a

code ranging from 1,000 "letters," or pairs of those chemical bases, to many hundreds of thousands. As if that weren't complex enough, the genes don't sit next to each other in a neat line but are broken up by lots of "junk" DNA known as an introns. As yet, scientists don't know what this junk is for.

The famous worm

In 1998, the first living creature to have its entire genome decoded was a tiny worm, *Caenorhabditis elegans*. It became world famous as a result! The following year, a team of scientists decoded chromosome 22, the second smallest of all human chromosomes. Here they found genes linked to cataracts in the eye and to mental illnesses such as schizophrenia.

A massive code

In June 2000, teams of scientists around the world finished decoding the human genome and made the results

A COMPLETE SET OF 23 PAIRS OF CHROMOSOMES FROM A SINGLE MALE CELL.

available over the internet. If it were typed up on sheets of 8 x 11 inch writing paper, it would fill 750,000 pages. Or, to put it another way, it is a single word looking like "ATATGCCGTA ATCG" and so on for more than 3 billion letters, the equivalent of 750 megabytes of data.

The truth about us
From this data, scientists have learned some startling facts. They now know that 98.9 percent of the human genome is junk DNA, and that genes make up a mere 1.1 percent! They also know that we possess between 30,000 and 40,000 genes per chromosome, not the 100,000 previously thought. The fruit fly has 13,000 genes per chromosome. When you consider that we're a lot bigger and smarter than fruit flies, this is truly bizarre! But the greatest consequence of mapping the genome is that scientists can now study the code gene by gene and work out what each does. In this way, cures for illnesses such as cancer might be possible in the years to come.

> WEIRD WORLD
> HUMANS HAVE 98.4 PERCENT OF DNA IN COMMON WITH CHIMPS, AND 30 PERCENT WITH LETTUCE!

IN THE FUTURE...

Predicting the future is always a risky business. Each generation tries to guess what's coming next, and usually fails to get it right. They said that space travel was impossible, world war would never happen twice, and computers would be too big and expensive for everyday use. Wrong every time. But in the strange world of codes, some predictions are likely to come true.

THIS IS THE CRAY 1 SUPERCOMPUTER. IT IS USED FOR NUCLEAR ATTACK SIMULATIONS AND STUDIES OF THE ATMOSPHERE.

Secrecy forever

It seems safe to predict that people will always need to keep secrets. It's also safe, therefore, to predict that people will always need codes. Can you imagine a world in which there were no secrets – no secret messages between friends, no spies or secret business deals?

Future codes

Codes will continue to get more complex. In the past, every new code seemed secure until someone found a way of cracking it. The Vigenère cipher seemed fail-safe, but Charles Babbage proved that it could be broken. Enigma, too, was invincible until Alan Turing set his mind to it. As a result, each new code invented is always more fiendishly difficult than the last. Supercomputers already exist that can perform calculations unimaginable only a few years ago. Who knows what new

key ciphers! In the future, however, it is possible that someone will work out a simple way to discover which two prime numbers make up a public key.

SUPERCOMPUTERS WILL MAKE AND BREAK FUTURE CODES

codes they may soon make or break?

Will any code be safe? When you spend money on the internet, the web browser sending your order uses its public key to encrypt the order. At the same time the company you're buying from uses its private key to receive the order. (Remember how Bob used Alice's public key? See page 69). At the moment, the public key encryption code described in that chapter is unbreakable. In fact, it would take all the computers on Earth longer than the age of the universe to break some large public

THIS NASA SUPERCOMPUTER IS USED TO MODEL A SPACECRAFT'S AEROBRAKING TECHNIQUES IN THE ATMOSPHERE OF MARS.

When that happens, the public key encryption code will no longer be safe and your order for two CDs could be used instead to steal all the money from your bank account!

Quantum computers

It's certain that computers will continue to play a major role in making and breaking codes. This seems obvious enough, since computers can handle huge calculations much faster than the human brain. But computers are only machines, and as with Enigma, codes made by machines can be broken by machines. That's why code makers are now interested in quantum theory.

The Danish scientist Niels Bohr said that *"anyone who can contemplate quantum mechanics without getting dizzy hasn't understood it."* He's right. Quantum theory is very, very hard to get your head around!

t states that tiny, subatomic particles, such as electrons and photons, behave in strange and unpredictable ways that do not obey the traditional laws of physics. This theory could be used to build a new generation of computers that do their calculations using these tiny particles. These quantum computers would be able to answer hundreds of questions at the same time and at a far faster rate than any supercomputer. Such machines could break all existing codes in seconds, including any public key encryption code.

particles sent down a fiber optic line. Each light particle vibrates in a different directi A message could be encoded using binary code and then transmitted by a series of lig particles. The different direction of ea particle's vibr v

PHOTONS TRANSMIT LIGHT. THEY ARE THE MOST COMMON PARTICLES IN THE UNIVERSE.

Quantum codes

Code makers could also use quantum theory to make codes that are absolutely unbreakable. Such codes could be based on the random behavior of light

represented by a binary number. Any attempt by a code breaker to in the particles would des the message. The code therefore be unbreaka It seems the future of quantum future

YOUR OWN CODES

There are hundreds of different ways to encode a message. If you want to make the grade as a secret agent, then practise using some of the following examples. They'll ensure that your private notes cannot be read by anyone. From the following, see what codes you can make from the simple phrase SECRETS IN A CODE. Then start writing your own messages...

Reverse groups
Form the letters into different groups, for example SEC RETSI NAC ODE. Then reverse the letters in each group –
CES ISTER CAN EDO.
You could then reverse the order of the groups –
EDO CAN ISTER CES.

Reverse random
Write the message backward –
EDOC A NI STERCES and then break the letters up into random new groups, for example ED OC AN IS TE RC ES or EDO CANISTER CES.

Mid-dummy
Break the message into even-numbered groups – SECR ET SINACO DE and then split each group in half: SE CR E T SIN ACO D E and insert a dummy letter into the middle of each group: SELCR EVT SINFACO DUE.

Bi-reverse
Break up the letters into pairs –
SE CR ET SI NA CO DE and then write each pair backward
– ES RC TE IS AN OC ED.

YOU MAY NEED TO FIND CLEVER WAYS OF CONCEALING YOUR SECRET MESSAGES. ONE SPY HID HIS IN A WALNUT!

You can also do this if the message can be evenly broken into groups of three, four, five, or more letters.

S andwich
Write out the first half of the message leaving a space between each letter – S E C R E T S and then write the second half in the spaces – SIENCARCEOTDSE. Then break up the coded message into smaller groups – SIEN CAR CEOTDSE.

EVEN A CAREFUL SEARCH WOULD BE UNLIKELY TO REVEAL THIS CODED MESSAGE WRITTEN ON THE UNDERSIDE OF A SMALL BUTTON DURING WORLD WAR I.

K eyword code
Write out the alphabet from A to Z. Underneath, write out a keyword, such as MOBILE, under the first six letters, and then add the rest of the alphabet in order, leaving

WITH THESE CODES YOUR SECRET NOTES WILL REMAIN JUST THAT!

C aesar shift
Move each letter three or more places down the alphabet. A therefore becomes D, B becomes E, and so on. Our message turns into VHFUHWV LQ D FRGH.

L etter swap
Here's a variation of the Caesar shift. Write out the alphabet from A to Z, and then under a letter near the end of the alphabet, say R, write the letter A. Then continue to write this lower alphabet until you get to Z in the upper alphabet and then start again under A.

out those letters you've used in your keyword.

V igenère cipher
Using the Vigenère cipher square on page 32, try to decipher the following famous quotation.
P IQPHAV EDEEGM PMCRUK WIVZKM CJQPIP EMZMVD I.
To help you decipher it (without having to do months of frequency analysis), the all-important keyword is PRIME. If you get stuck, you can find the answer at the bottom of the next page.

Number code

Write out the alphabet and give each letter a number, starting with whatever number you like and increasing in ones or twos or threes. A could therefore equal 3, B could equal 6, C 9, and so on.

Calender code

Write out the letters of the alphabet in a row and number

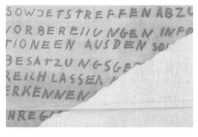

SOME SPIES WRITE THEIR CODES IN INVISIBLE INK FOR EXTRA SECURITY. THIS ONE WAS WRITTEN ON A HANDKERCHIEF.

the letters 1–26. Then write out our message, "secrets in a code" using the numbers you've given them: 19.5.3.18.5.20.19.9.14.1. 3.15.4.5. Now choose any calendar month and give each day of the week an initial: M, T_1, W, T_2, F, S_1, S_2. (More than one day of the week begins with T and S, so Sunday, for example, becomes S_2.)

To encode our message, start at the beginning with 19: if the 19th day of the month falls on the third Wednesday, give it

the code W3. If the 5th day falls on the first Thursday, 5 becomes $T_2$1, and so on for the rest of the message. To decode a calendar-coded message, reverse the process by turning the codes back into days of the month and then into letters and words. Obviously, both you and the sender need to know what month and year you're in!

Vowel code

Write out the letters of the alphabet in a row, and number the vowels 1 to 5, so that A = 1, E = 2, I = 3, O = 4, and U = 5. Each consonant is then coded according to the number of letters it is to the right of the nearest vowel. S is 4 letters to the right of O (vowel number 4), so becomes 44, E is vowel 2, C is two letters from A, so becomes 12, and so on. Place a period between the numbers to separate them: 44.2.12.43.2. 45.44.3.35.1.13.4.14.2 is our message in code.

Vigenère cipher answer

Using the keyword PRIME, you should have discovered that the well-known quotation is "A riddle wrapped in a mystery inside an enigma." It was actually said by Winston Churchill about Russia in October 1939, seven months before he became prime minister of the Great Britain.

REFERENCE SECTION

Whether you've finished reading *Code Breakers*, or are turning to this section first, you'll find the information on the next eight pages really useful. Here are more codes, historical facts, and all the terms a code breaker needs to know. You'll find a list of website addresses too. So, whether you want to surf the net or search out facts, these pages should turn you from an enthusiast into an expert.

MORSE CODE

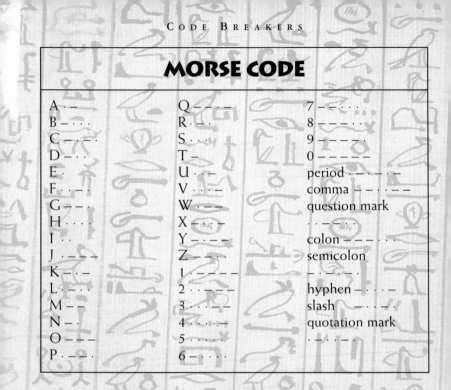

A ·—	Q ——·—	7 ——·· ·
B —···	R ·—·	8 ———··
C —·—·	S ···	9 ————·
D —··	T —	0 —————
E ·	U ··—	period ·—·—·—
F ··—·	V ···—	comma ——··——
G ——·	W ·——	question mark
H ····	X —··—	··——··
I ··	Y —·——	colon ———···
J ·———	Z ——··	semicolon
K —·—	1 ·————	—·—·—·
L ·—··	2 ··———	hyphen —····—
M ——	3 ···——	slash —··—·
N —·	4 ····—	quotation mark
O ———	5 ·····	·—··—·
P ·——·	6 —····	

THE PIGPEN CIPHER

The pigpen cipher has been used since the 1700s to keep records safe and is still in use today. It substitutes individual letters with symbols, according to where each letter lies on a grid. The message "secrets in a code" is encrypted below using the pigpen symbols.

Letters on a grid

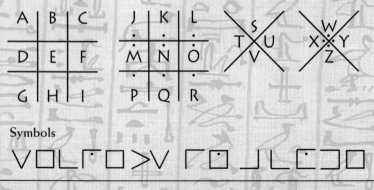

Symbols

NAVAJO CODE

NAVAJO MILITARY CODE WORDS

English word	Navajo word	Literal Translation
Formations		
Corps	DIN-NEH-IH	Clan
Division	ASHIH-HI	Salt
Regiment	TABAHA	Edge water
Battalion	TACHEENE	Red soil
Company	NAKIA	Mexican
Platoon	HAS-CLISH-NIH	Mud
Section	YO-IH	Beads
Squad	DEBEH-LI-ZINI	Black sheep
Officers		
General	BIH-KEH-HE	War chief
Major general.	SO-NA-KIH	Two star
Brigadier general	SO-A-LA-IH	One star
Lt. colonel	CHE-CHIL-BE-TAH-BESH-LEGAI	Silver oak leaf
Colonel	ATSAH-BESH-LE-GAI	Silver eagle
Captain	BESH-LEGAI-NAH-KIH	Two silver bars
Lieutenant	BESH-LEGAI-A-LAH-IH	One silver bar
Executive officer	BIH-DA-HOL-NEHI	Those in charge
Countries		
Alaska	BEH-HGA	With winter
Australia	CHA-YES-DESI	Rolled hat
Britain	TOH-TA	Between waters
China	CEH-YEHS-BESI	Braided hair
France	DA-GHA-HI	Beard
Germany	BESH-BE-CHA-HE	Iron hat
Iceland	TKIN-KE-YAH	Ice land
India	AH-LE-GAI	White clothes
Italy	DOH-HA-CHI-YALI-TCHI	Stutter
Philippines	KE-YAH-DA-NA-LHE	Floating island
Russia	SILA-GOL-CHI-IH	Red army
Spain	DEBA-DE-NIH	Sheep pain
United States	NE-HE-MAH	Our mother

contd/...

Airplanes

Planes	WO-TAH-DE-NE-IH	Air force
Dive bomber	GINI	Chicken hawk
Torpedo plane	TAS-CHIZZIE	Swallow
Observation plane	NE-AS-JAH	Owl
Fighter plane	DA-HE-TIH-HI	Hummingbird
Bomber plane	JAY-SHO	Buzzard
Patrol plane	GA-GIH	Crow
Transport	ATSAH	Eagle

Ships

Ships	TOH-DINEH-IH	Sea force
Battleship	LO-TSO	Whale
Aircraft	TSIDI-MOFFA-YE-HI	Bird carrier
Submarine	BESH-LO	Iron fish
Minesweeper	CHA	Beaver
Destroyer	CA-LO	Shark
Transport	DINEH-NAY-YE-HI	Man carrier
Cruiser	LO-TSO-YAZZIE	Small whale

Months

January	ATSAH-BE-YAZ	Small eagle
February	WOZ-CHEIND	Squeeky voice
March	TAH-CHILL	Small plant
April	TAH-TSO	Big plant
May	TAH-TSOSIE	Small plant
June	BE-NE-EH-EH-JAH-TSO	Big planting
July	BE-NE-TA-TSOSIE	Small harvest
August	BE-NEEN-TA-TSO	Big harvest
September	GHAW-JIH	Half
October	NIL-CHI-TSOSIE	Small wind
November	NIL-CHI-TSO	Big wind
December	YAS-NIL-TES	Crusted snow

General terms

Artillery	BE-AL-DOH-TSO-LANI	Many big guns
Bombs	A-YE-SHI	Eggs
Camp	TO-ALTSEH-HOGAN	Temporary place
Force	TA-NA-NE-LADI	Without care
Grenades	NI-MA-SI	Potatoes
Machine gun	A-KNAH-AS-DONIH	Rapid fire gun
Rocket	LESZ-YIL-BESHI	Sand boil
Sailor	CHA-LE-GAI	White caps
Tank	CHAY-DA-GAHI	Tortoise

FAMOUS CODE BREAKERS

Leon Battista Alberti
1404–72
An Italian architect, musician, and artist, Alberti also had a passion for secret writing. He invented a rotating alphabetical disc, which was a major advancement in code making. The disc's larger and smaller plates shifted alignment to put letters into code. He also devised a new form of cipher that used two or more cipher alphabets at the same time and switched between them from letter to letter. This idea was later refined by Vigenère.

Charles Babbage
1791–1887
Babbage was a British inventor famous for creating the forerunner of the modern computer. In the 1820s and '30s, Babbage built two Difference Engines, which could be programmed to make advanced mathematical calculations. In 1854 he proved that the Vigenère cipher could be broken using frequency analysis.

Étienne Bazeries
1846–1931
A French army code breaker, Bazeries was famous for cracking Louis XIV's Great Cipher. In doing so he revealed the likely identity of the famous man in the iron mask. Bazeries also invented a wheel cipher machine similar to Thomas Jefferson's.

Jean-François Champollion
1790–1832
A Frenchman with great expertise in ancient languages, Champollion was the first to decode Egyptian hieroglyphs completely. He unlocked the ancient language by comparing the royal names written in Greek and in hieroglyphs that were carved on the Rosetta Stone.

Francis Crick 1916–
James Watson 1928–
These men discovered the double-helix shape of DNA. This enabled scientists to understand human genetics and eventually to decipher the human genetic code. They were jointly awarded the Nobel Prize for medicine in 1962.

Agnes Driscoll
1889–1971
Driscoll worked in US Naval Intelligence after World War I, where she became a first-rate code breaker nicknamed "Madame X." In 1936 she broke the codes of a Japanese spy network operating in the US and by the outbreak of World War II she was regularly breaking Japanese naval codes.

Rosalind Franklin
1920–58
Franklin was a British physicist who proved that DNA molecules were spiral in shape. Her discovery led to the eventual breaking of the human genetic code.

William Friedman
1891–1969

Friedman taught code breaking to the US Army before World War II. His greatest achievement was to break the Japanese Purple cipher in 1940. Friedman also wrote a series of scientific papers that set out the basics of modern code breaking and linked it to sound mathematical principles.

Thomas Jefferson
1743–1826

The third president of the US, and principal draftsman of the Declaration of Independence, Jefferson also invented a 36-wheel cipher machine. The machine was eventually adopted by the US military 100 years after Jefferson invented it!

Al-Kindi
9th century AD

Al-Kindi was an Arab scholar who wrote the *Manuscript on Deciphering Cryptographic Messages*. In this work, which was only rediscovered in 1987, he outlined the principles of frequency analysis. This is a method for cracking codes by working out how frequently letters appear in both the ciphertext and the original language of the plaintext.

Marian Rejewski
1905–80

Rejewski was a Polish code breaker who cracked the prewar versions of the Enigma code. Rejewski built replica Enigma machines, known as bombes, to test the various scrambler arrangements. His work was passed on to Alan Turing and other code breakers at Bletchley Park at the start of World War II.

Antoine Rossignol
1600–82

France's first full-time code breaker, Rossignol held a high position in the court of Louis XIV and played a major role in shaping French diplomacy. He invented the king's Great Cipher, which remained unbroken until the 19th century. The word *rossignol* became French slang for a lockpick, a testament to Rossignol's skill at unlocking ciphers.

Arthur Scherbius
1878–1929

The Enigma machine was the brainchild of this German inventor. The first machines were manufactured in 1923, originally to protect commercial secrets, but soon Enigma was used exclusively by the German military.

Alan Turing
1912–54

Turing was the British mathematician who cracked the advanced wartime version of the Enigma code. This enabled the Allies to read most German military secrets. In 1937 Turing outlined plans for the Universal Turing Machine, an early version of today's computers. Today he is considered to be one of the world's finest ever computer scientists.

Michael Ventris
1922–56
Ventris was a British architect with a fascination for ancient history. He was also a talented linguist and set himself the task of deciphering Linear B, the mysterious script of ancient Crete. Linear B was thought to be a unique, lost language, but Ventris proved that it was in fact a very early form of Greek, causing historians to rewrite the history books.

Blaise de Vigenère
1523–96
Vigenère was a French diplomat who learned the art of cryptography while on diplomatic missions to Rome. His complex cipher uses 26 separate cipher alphabets arranged in a square, the so-called Vigenère square. It remained unbreakable for nearly 300 years.

Thomas Young
1773–1829
A British scholar, Thomas Young was the first to realize that some Egyptian hieroglyphs represented single letters and sounds, just like a modern alphabet. His work allowed Champollion to decipher hieroglyphs completely a few years later.

CODE AND CIPHER WEBSITES

www.channel4.com/plus/secrecy/
Excellent general website covering many of the codes in this book.
http://codebreaker.dids.com/
General website introducing code breaking for the young beginner.
www.trincoll.edu/depts/cpsc/cryptography/caesar.html
A clear site that explains how to break a Caesar shift.
http://ccat.sas.upenn.edu/~jmcgill/abletter.html
Babington's deciphered letter to Mary, Queen of Scots.
www.nsa.gov/museum/
The US National Security Agency website that is dedicated to the history of American code breaking.

http://frode.home.cern.ch/frode/crypto/index.html
A vast site offering hundreds of links to sites on every aspect of codes, ciphers, and cryptology.
http://homepages.tesco.net/~andy carlson/enigma/enigma_j.html
A virtual Enigma keyboard, complete with scrambler rotors, that enciphers your messages.
www.codesandciphers.org.uk/
Detailed website with pictures of the Enigma and Lorenz machines.
www.turing.org.uk/turing/
A website dedicated to Alan Turing's life and work.
www.sanger.ac.uk/HGP
Technical but fascinating DNA site with everything you need to know about chromosomes.

GLOSSARY

Binary code
The code used by computers consisting of two digits, 0 and 1.

Black chambers
Secret code-breaking offices that intercepted mail.

Bletchley Park
The British World War II code-breaking center, where the Enigma cipher was broken.

Book cipher
A cipher where the key is to be found in the numbered words of a particular book. The first letter of the first word is 1, the first letter of the second word is 2, and so on.

Caesar shift
An ancient cipher in which each letter of the alphabet is substituted with another letter one, two, or more places further down the alphabet.

Cipher
A system for hiding the meaning of a message by replacing each letter with another letter. A cipher is usually deciphered with a key.

Ciphertext
The text of a message after it has been enciphered.

Code
A system for hiding the meaning of a message by replacing whole words or phrases with a letter, number, or symbol (or sets of them) listed in a codebook. Also used in a general sense to mean any code or cipher.

Codebook
A book containing a list of replacements for words or phrases in the original message.

Cryptanalysis
The breaking of a code or cipher.

Cryptography
The act of putting a message into a code or cipher. Cryptography and cryptanalysis together make up the science of cryptology, the study of codes and ciphers.

Cuneiform
Wedge-shaped picture writing used in ancient Mesopotamia.

Day key
A special cipher used to encipher and decipher one day's messages.

Decipher
To turn the enciphered message back into the original message.

Decode
To turn an encoded message back into the original message.

Decrypt
To decipher or decode a message.

Encipher
To turn the original message into an enciphered message.

Encode
To turn the original message into the encoded message.

Encrypt
To encipher or encode a message.

Enigma
A German World War II machine that enciphered messages through a complex system of rotating scramblers.

Frequency analysis
A system of code breaking that compares the number of times a letter or symbol is used in a coded

message with the letters used most frequently in the language in which the cipher was originally written.

Genetic code
The blueprint for human life contained in genes inside our chromosomes.

Glyph
A form of pictogram, used by the Maya and others in the Americas.

Hieroglyph
A form of picture writing used in ancient Egypt.

Heliograph
A day-time signaling device that uses reflected sunlight.

Human genome
The entire genetic code or makeup of the human body.

Key
A special code, consisting of numbers, a word, a short phrase, or even a book, known to both the sender and receiver of an enciphered message. The key allows the receiver to decipher the message.

Message key
A special cipher used to encipher and decipher a single message.

Morse code
A code for use via telegraph. It consists of a series of electrical pulses – dots and dashes. Each combination represents a letter of the alphabet.

Navajo
The language of the Native American Navajo tribe used as a code during World War II.

Pictogram
A picture representing a word or idea.

Plaintext
The original message before

it has been enciphered.

Private key
The key used by the receiver to decipher a message using public-key cryptography. A private key must be kept secret.

Public key
The key used by the sender to encipher a message using public-key cryptography.

Public-key cryptography
A system of cryptography that uses different keys at either end – a public key to encipher a message, a private key to decipher it.

Purple machine
A Japanese World War II machine that enciphered messages through a system of telephone switches.

Quantum code
A cipher based on the random behavior of subatomic particles.

Quantum computer
A future computer that would operate with subatomic particles.

Scytale
An early form of transposed cipher.

Semaphore
A signaling code using flags or arms to represent letters.

Short Message Service
The formal name for text messaging.

Text messaging
Sending an abbreviated message by mobile phone.

Vigenère square
A cipher that consists of 26 separate alphabets arranged in a square.

Wheel-cipher
Two or more rotating alphabetical discs, fixed together, that shift alignment to encrypt letters.

INDEX

CREDITS

Dorling Kindersley would like to thank:
Marcus James for the initial design concept and Chris Bernstein for compiling the index.

The author would like to thank:
David Broom for his technical know-how and Fran, Stefan, Darren, and especially David at DK for all their help and support with the writing, editing, and design of the book.
